D1624081

A Few Flowers For My Soul:

A Gardener's View of the Healing Power of Cut Flowers

A Few Flowers For My Soul:

A Gardener's View of the Healing Power of Cut Flowers

Robbie Williams

Best Wishes,
Cheers!
Robbie Williams

HH
HARBOR
HOUSE

Augusta, Georgia

A Few Flowers For My Soul:
A Gardener's View of the Healing Power of Cut Flowers
By Robbie Williams
A Harbor House Book/2007

Copyright 2007 by Robbie Williams

All rights reserved. No part of this book may be reproduced or transmitted in any form or by any means, electronic or mechanical, including photocopying, recording, or by any information storage and retrieval system, without permission in writing from the publisher.

For information address:
>   HARBOR HOUSE
>   111 TENTH STREET
>   AUGUSTA, GA 30901
Cover design and back cover photo by Jenifer Parkman
Jacket and book design by Nathan Elliott
Insert photos by Glenn J. Bridges
Front cover photo by Susannah Bridges
Illustration by Lee Heffernan

Library of Congress Cataloging-in-Publication Data
Williams, Robbie, 1937-
  A few flowers for my soul : a gardener's view of the healing power of cut flowers/ Robbie Williams.
      p. cm.
 ISBN 978-1-891799-74-7
 1. Flowers--Therapeutic use. I. Title.
 RX615.F555W55 2007
 615.8'515--dc22
                              2007004334

10 9 8 7 6 5 4 3 2 1

For Harriett…

And all of the other "Harrietts" of the world who make living in a small town fun and give it special meaning.

Contents

What is a cut flower?

Dictionary Definition: Any of various kinds of showy, fresh flowers used in arrangements

My Definition: Any fresh flower that is cut from outside and brought inside for the purpose of adoration, meditation and healing

CR&O

MANY PEOPLE FAIL to realize the importance of having fresh flowers inside—where these beauties can be enjoyed at night and early in the morning. Sitting before a simple vase of fresh cut flowers and admiring their color, form, and even fragrance, if they have any, is indeed a worthwhile pastime. The kitchen window over the sink, the bathroom vanity where the toothbrush is resting, the bedside table—these are all places to adore the fresh cut flower. Taking time to carefully observe every aspect of the bloom has a healing effect on the soul and gives the soul time to mend from its every hurt.

 CREA

THE STORIES IN this book are based on some of the experiences I have had from the growing and marketing cut flowers, as well as from meeting some unusual people who bought these flowers. Some actual persons' names have been changed to protect their identity, but their feelings and emotions are the real thing.

CRED

I WOULD LIKE to thank all of the people who allowed me to write about them in this book. My special thanks go to Peggy Cheney, Editor Extraordinaire, without whom my characters would not shine nearly so brightly. She possesses a special talent in editing that resembles mothering rather than just adding and correcting phrases. One might say she loves a manuscript into its best form.

Preface

The British naturalist Charles Darwin turned the world of biology upside down in 1859 when he published his *Origin of Species*, in which he put forth the theory of evolution. But even before him, his grandfather, Erasmus Darwin, a physician, scientist and poet, had published a poem called "Zoomania" in which he foretold of the coming events of his grandson's theories. The argument has gone on for many, many years—that argument about man evolving from animals. There have been church controversies, legal wranglings and personal upheavals as a result of the Darwinian theories, and there is still a question mark in many minds today. However, I have a theory different from the one these men hold. I think that if there is an evolutionary process, people probably come from flowering plants, not from animals. And on what scientific data do I base my theory? Why, none. But, I have made the following observation: Certain people are like certain flowers. Not only do they resemble these flowers in personality, but also they seem to be attracted to them in a rather strange way.

So after spending years growing, cutting, arranging and admiring flowers, I decided to put down in writing some of my theories of not necessarily flower evolution, but the power of flowers on people's personalities. After all, since the beginning of time, there has been a love affair between people and flowers, making me think that there must be some sort of familial connection between the two. I don't know about you, but I rather like thinking that I came from some sort of lovely flower, rather than from a gorilla. After all, flowers seem to me to have a more direct route to God than any sort of ape or monkey. Therefore, I choose to think that I came from this Divine Maker through some primitive, beautiful flower, and that's as scientific as this book gets. This is not to discredit the value of science, but rather to make my case for the priceless value of the beauty and comfort that flowers bring to us all.

I do sincerely believe in the healing power of fresh cut flowers because I have seen too many examples of this power over the years when I have gone to funerals, visited the sick, or watched the expression on a young child's face when he is given just one bloom. An old lady in a nursing home can shed a tear of appreciation by simply looking at a few flowers in her small room without a view. When you have traveled where I have been with flowers, taking time to "smell the roses" will take on a whole new meaning. Flowers are truly food for the soul.

Part 1

Dublin

"I'll Bet You Are Not From Here, Are You?"

Glenn and I were asked that question hundreds of times by both strangers and friends in our new central Georgia rural area. Before coming here, we were unaware that when someone moves within the same state from a different town and a different life, the locals are always able to pick up on the fact that the new resident is not native to their area. Looking back, I can see the perfect reasoning for this question, but at the time, we were totally unaware of how much we stood out in the midst of these natives. Georgia is a rather large state in which different cultures and customs dictate the everyday life of three sections, with imaginary lines forming the North Georgia section, the Middle Georgia section, and the South Georgia section. Moving across the line from North Georgia to Middle Georgia caused us to be viewed by most locals as a little like aliens. This obvious unnatural appearance of the two of us would prompt conversation among all kinds of people and circumstances. The checkout clerk at the grocery store, the hairdresser, the tax assessor and the newfound friend were all on the same page as far as this question-asking proposition was concerned. So we were constantly explaining just how we happened to find ourselves located here in an area where we did not exactly look like or act like we had lived here all of our lives. We were not the ones who in any way felt out of place or even dislocated, but rather the natives' impressions of us created this need to ask, "I'll bet you are not from here, are you?" As a matter of fact, we felt right at home in our new situation. But there was and is a need to explain the route that took us from other sections of the state to the Middle Georgia area. This is the path we took and an explanation of the way we ended up at the ranch:

Many years ago, something like forty or fifty, Glenn and I had dated for a short time while he was a senior medical student and I was working as a medical technologist for a pathologist in Augusta, Georgia. It was not a serious relationship, nor was it lengthy, but it was a fun time for both of us. And then, he went far away to do additional training and I married someone else. For a period of thirty-some years, there was no contact between the two of us. During this thirty-year period of my marriage, I had given birth to and reared three daughters in Augusta. My oldest daughter, after college graduation and a short, three-year marriage, moved to Atlanta and began working for a large television network there, moving up the corporate ladder with exceptional speed. She, from time to time, was plagued with urinary tract infections and called me one day to say that she needed to see a doctor about this problem. She said that she had called our local urologist's office in Augusta and gotten the names of five doctors in the Atlanta area. She explained that the first one on the list was taking no new patients, the second one was out of town, the third one had no openings for several weeks, and the fourth one had a medical problem and was away from his practice, but the fifth doctor's receptionist told her that they could see her the next day. Her question to me was "Do you think something is funny about this, and would it be safe for me to see him?" I explained that maybe he just had a cancellation, or maybe he just ran a rather efficient office, and she could always get a second opinion after she saw him, if she were unhappy with him. And so she went to see him. When she walked into his office, he said, "Lee, I think I used to boogie with your mother in medical school!!!" Lee was a little more than overwhelmed. Sure enough—here was the Glenn from thirty years ago.

Sometimes there really isn't an explanation for the way Fate orchestrates the events on its calendar, and we humans are left to try to figure it out as we go along life's bumpy road, which is already loaded with surprises that mimic hidden land mines of the worst kind. So while Lee saw Glenn for her malady, Glenn and I had reason to rehash old stories and speak briefly about the events of the last thirty years. I found that he was in a nineteen-year marriage, which had dwindled to a rather unpleasant state over the years, and he was trying to find a solution to get out of it. This scenario matched a situation of my own, and as a result we found that we had much more in common than just the past. Our respective divorces that followed, some time later, were just as horrible as all the stories that circulate about the bad "D" word. However, after a few years filled with pain and suffering, some doors were finally closed, and our lives seemed to be headed in a new direction, a direction that led us to Middle Georgia.

Glenn decided to leave his private practice of twenty-five years to accept a position at the VA Medical Center in Dublin, Georgia, and I stayed in Atlanta, where I had been living since a couple of years before his move to central Georgia. Needless to say, there was a lot of driving between the two towns, and after a time, I decided to leave the big city and get a place in this peaceful town where Glenn now lived. Given our past experiences with marriage, we did not want to enter into any contracts that might prevent us from enjoying our cherished freedom. So we continued to be near each other as the best of friends, but not bound by any kind of paper agreement.

So I came to the city of Dublin to be near my old friend

and to get away from the fast lifestyle of Atlanta. It was a little like coming home since I had grown up in a similar small town not too far from this community. I rented a small house and began to look for some kind of work—work that eventually included being a front desk receptionist, transcriptionist and golf instructor. That is the story of "I'll bet you are not from here."

"The Land Is So Ugly Our Hunting Club Doesn't Want It"

After settling in at the hospital, Glenn took on the mission of trying to find some land outside the small town, a place where he could at last be a play-like farmer of sorts and where neighbors were not close by. Farming had been something he had had an interest in since the age of sixteen when his family had experienced a failed attempt at this kind of endeavor. Anyway, the big city atmosphere of Atlanta had left him with a burning desire to live someplace where curtains were not necessary for the windows and neighbors were so far away that the lights from their houses could not be seen at night. Buying this piece of land proved to be much more difficult than he had expected. He found not only that the average person did not have any available land for sale, but also that the large land owners were looking for even more land to add to their already huge acreage. This particular county seemed to have a few families with vast amounts of land, and this land had been in their families for generations, making the breakup of the land parcels next to impossible. Glenn was finally reduced to asking not only realtors and people in the business of marketing land, but also the average man on the street, and he even started to ask

20

patients in his Tuesday clinic at the hospital. The two of us drove many miles around the county looking for any signs of land for sale. In fact, we probably grew to know more about the rural area surrounding this town than the locals because every free moment was spent chasing down some fruitless clue about an acre of land that did not exist.

Glenn's big break finally came on a certain Tuesday at one of those clinics I mentioned. One of his patients who had had that question about land posed to him several times came into the clinic for his regular checkup and asked if Glenn would like to look at some land out in a Mennonite community about twelve miles from town. In this area of Georgia, there were several communities of these religious people who seemed to ban together, often owning houses and land within close range of each other. All of these people and their farms were located near their church, which dictated that they dress a certain way and live by their church's strict rules. These Mennonites—particularly the women—could be recognized by their unusual customs and mode of dress. The dark hose, the small white cap on the back of the pinned-up hair, the loose-fitting cotton dress and the lack of makeup were all signs that these devout women put their religion first on their priority list. All the residents of Dublin had seen these people in town and were familiar with their communities, often going to their farms to purchase fresh produce and baked goods. The clinic patient further explained that his hunting club had been out to take a look at the property and had turned it down because it was even too ugly for hunting. This assessment of the property did not deter Glenn. In fact, he was even more interested in it as a result of the patient's comment. His interest was further kindled when the patient explained that the owner was in some kind of financial difficulty because of the low price of pork. The land was presently being used or had in the past been used for a pig farm. In Glenn's mind the wheels were rolling: ugly land and financial problems added up to a piece of land he could possibly afford, not to mention the availability of the land, something quite extinct he had found as a result of his long search. The patient gave Glenn the owner's phone number and address, and it took Glenn only a matter of minutes to get in touch with him and arrange a meeting. In fact, that afternoon Glenn was riding up the pig trail to the top of the property, looking around and envisioning how to make this his dream place, hoping that he could somehow make this ugly land his. His first look at this place that was to become "Chinaberry Ranch" did nothing to diminish his dream of all the possibilities he had in mind for it. Glenn considered himself very lucky, but in my opinion, this former pig farm was lucky to have a prospective owner whose vision was not clouded with what he saw. His futile search for land and his need to fulfill his plan for some kind of farm project combined to cover his mind with all kinds of wonderful visions of all his pent-up projects from long ago. All those projects and plans he had had since he was a young boy came flooding back across his mind, and he could see only beautiful possibilities on this ugly land. The unattractiveness of this place did not even register with him, partly because of his long search, but mainly because he was able to go way beyond the present view to a place in the future where it bore no resemblance to its present conditions. What some might have thought was impossible, he took on as a challenge, but not just any challenge—this challenge was to be his and his alone. There would be no large crews of workmen out cutting down trees, clearing the land, moving dirt and making it into a workable place. He envisioned himself up on that tractor doing most of the work. There would be no experts making the place a thing of beauty. He wanted to have a hand in every action that led to the completion of the place. On that first afternoon when Glenn saw the Mennonite pig farm, he mentally was able to know the place would be the answer to his prayers—a country place that he could almost by himself carve out, dig, hoe, build, transform, and most of all "love" into shape.

Chinaberry Ranch

The first time I saw the property that was to become Chinaberry Ranch, I could not believe my eyes. It was quite possibly the ugliest piece of land I had ever seen. A couple of years before my first visit, the property had been used for a pig farm, and since that time, it had been left to the desires of all kinds of weeds, brush, vines and small trees. I could almost imagine how God felt when He first started with the Garden of Eden. The small, winding dirt road that led to the top of the hill was a single lane wide and a red clay disaster that was almost impassable. Our car could hardly make it through the bramble and briars that grew alongside the road and almost covered the top of the car windows. Glenn assured me that he thought the place had great possibilities—he was a man with vision. About halfway up the hill, I began to think that possibly his vision must have been severely impaired because this place could never be anything but unattractive in my eyes.

Finally the car made it to the part of the hill that should have been the top, but because we could not open the car doors, it was impossible to really know exactly where we were. The brush and undergrowth covered everything.

However, we could just barely discern the outline of a long tin roof, so we knew that under that there must be a barn or a barn-like structure. Later we would know that it had been the farrowing house for the pigs when there was a pig farm here. Naturally, I did not know what a farrowing house was, but I would come to know that it is the place where baby pigs are born. When we did push the doors open enough to have limited views around the place, I immediately jumped back into the car because I knew there was a good possibility that some unfriendly snakes might have set up housekeeping under all that brush. I certainly did not want to interfere with whatever they had going at that time. Glenn was not as worried as I about the "shoulderless ones," and he even walked, or should I say pushed, through some of the weeds and brush to find a long concrete pad, which, we would later learn, was used as a place to feed the pigs.

We did not stay very long because, after all, there was little to see. As a result of this visit, Glenn decided the first step would be to hire a man with a bulldozer to clear some of the place. I thought this sounded like a good idea, but I did not envy the man his job. It seemed insurmountable to me. And sure enough he came, and after three tries, several breakdowns with his bulldozer and long, tedious hours, he was able to clear a small piece of land on top of the hill.

On my second visit to the property, I could not decide if the place looked better covered with the brush or naked with all the bare red clay ruts shining in the sun. The pig ruts, the packed hard clay and the absence of grass everywhere made the place look like a nuclear disaster had just occurred. But Glenn insisted again that the place had possibilities. I still had my doubts.

The next step was getting a tractor. Glenn decided a tractor would allow him the means to move dirt, clear small brush and generally feel like a real countryman. With this man, it's never just as simple as purchasing the needed item. The search and the research make the buying process a thing of joy. He can spend hundreds of hours looking in trade magazines, talking to other owners of the product and calling all over the country to find out any information that he could put in his vast storehouse of knowledge about the proposed purchase. It became abundantly clear to me that some of the tedious fact-finding might just be a maneuver to postpone the decision-making process. After all, making a final decision and facing up to a commitment are cousins of a sort, and men generally find these are rather uncomfortable situations in which to be.

The tractor buying adventure started with, of all things, my Saab. For about ten years, my Saab had been maintained by numerous service departments and general mechanics around the state. Much to my amazement, I found just a few miles from Glenn's new property a jewel of a guy whose only passion in life was working on all kinds of automobiles, even the imported kind. Every now and then, a man comes along who is not interested in any hobby or sporting event, doesn't own a boat or airplane, and even forgoes gardening and volunteer work. Such a man was Bruce. His love of cars had begun when he was just a small boy and continued to grow with the boy on into manhood. A car could not have a better friend.

Before many changes happened at the newly purchased property, my Saab needed to be repaired. So Glenn and I took the car over to Bruce's repair shop for an assessment of the car's problems. Of course, Glenn had his ongoing project about the purchase of a tractor milling around in the caverns of his mind and was always looking for any way to increase his inventory of information. After a brief discussion about my Saab, Glenn asked Bruce if he knew anyone who might have a used tractor for sale in the area. Because the shop was located in the middle of a big farming region, it seemed a logical place to continue the tractor search. Bruce replied that just a short distance from his shop was a rather unusual man who had recently completely restored an old tractor.

He further explained that not only had this man restored the tractor, but he had also added a front-end loader and some other special equipment. In addition, he had painted and prettied up the machine to be a thing of exceptional beauty. Bruce told us to visit this man named Prescott, assuring us that he would be happy to show us his tractor creation. He also added that maybe Prescott could help us find a nice used tractor. As fast as Glenn's car would take us, we sped away. The search and research were on.

Prescott's neat and attractive house sat right on the country road, a paved road, but rather far from the local town. In the distance behind this house was a group of other small buildings and wood frame houses. This whole setting resembled a community of sorts with various activities taking place there. The lawns and shrubbery were trimmed and well kept, and all the buildings seemed freshly painted. While standing there waiting for the door to be answered, we had the feeling that someone who loved perfect maintenance was in charge here. Glenn never seemed to have a problem presenting himself to a perfect stranger. However, I felt a little uncomfortable standing on the porch of someone I had never met, hoping to ask for information about a possession of his. All of my apprehensions were assuaged when a personable man around forty-five or fifty years of age answered the door. He greeted us with a smile even before we had a chance to introduce ourselves and state our mission. When we explained that Bruce had told us about his "pretty" tractor, his smile became even wider and he grew very excited. He said he would be very pleased to show us his creation and quickly led us to the rear of the property to see the tractor.

A beautiful shade of blue filled our eyes when we looked in the direction of the huge tractor. The setting sun cast shadows across the machine and gave it an almost mystical look. After all, a tractor is supposed to be big, gross and most of all, slightly dirty. This tractor was not only a beautiful shade of blue but also shiny and clean as a whistle. Prescott explained that he had purchased the tractor at an auction of state highway equipment some time ago, and he had spent long hours making the big monster into his own creation. Glenn had been circling the tractor and making small groans with each circle, as he turned green with envy. I could almost see his brain turning around an image of himself riding high on a machine like this and him feeling like he could conquer the wildness of his newly purchased property. He finally asked Prescott if he knew where he could get a tractor like this one, a used one to refurbish and modify for his needs. Prescott assured him that he would certainly keep his eyes open for any upcoming auctions or equipment sales in the area and promised to call him if he came across a good machine at a good price.

As we made our way back to the front of the property, Glenn explained that he had just purchased some land not too far from there and needed to get a tractor to help with the clearing of the brush and woods. He mentioned that he would need to see about a small house to move onto the property later. At this point, Prescott loudly exclaimed that one of the small wood frame houses on his property had belonged to his mother-in-law, and she had just died. The house was vacant and he would like to sell it. When the question of how the house might be moved came up, Prescott said, "No problem—I can do that!" I was beginning to think that this Prescott was the champion jack-of-all-trades. Later I would find that my first impression was totally correct

After two or three more visits to Prescott's house, Glenn bought the small "mother-in-law" house and arranged to have the moving done by the seller and some of his friends. One of the friends happened to be in the junk business and was the proud owner of several junk wreckers and an old yellow school bus, which the junk dealer had converted into an "RV" of sorts. Without explaining too thoroughly, Prescott made us believe the house could be moved rather easily with these wreckers and school buses. Plans were made to move the house during lunchtime so, in Prescott's words, the "State Patrol will be eating and we won't get caught without a permit." And that is exactly what happened. The house made it to the property without too many problems, except for some broken power lines, a few downed mailboxes and some stalled traffic. All of these problems got solved with some smooth talking and innocent finagling by Prescott, and the house was brought to rest at the bottom of the red clay hill. This is where it remained for several weeks because some torrential rains came about this time, and the ground was so slick nothing, could make it up the hill.

The small house was not extremely attractive in its original setting, but as it sat in its new location at the bottom of the red clay hill, it looked even more pitiful. We had ample time to look at this atrocity and wonder what would possess anyone in his right mind to make such a purchase. It had some kind of dirty blue shingles on the sides, an uneven tin roof, only a few windows, and no personality at all. As it continued to sit there for some time, it was almost as if someone were trying to make us realize just how foolish we had been to purchase this little monster. But our sense of humor saved us. We would visit the little blue house and make all kinds of jokes about it, take funny photographs of it, and generally confirm our belief that something worthwhile would come of it.

The sun finally came out, the road dried out, and it was time to move the house to the top of the hill. At this point, the trouble was just beginning. We had come up with the idea of elevating the house so that we would have a nice view of the surrounding land and an exceptional view of the sky. We decided that if the house were put on some kind of foundation like concrete blocks and raised eight feet into the air, we would have a rather nice view, something that is unheard of in this area. Everyone else's house sat directly on the dirt surrounded by a pine forest or lots of enormous trees and shrubbery, making a view of the sky virtually impossible. Maybe it was because we had no trees to speak of anyway that we decided to settle for having a view of the distant forest and the open sky. To say that we had no trees isn't exactly correct. When the land was cut over and all the nice trees were taken by the loggers, a few chinaberry trees stalwartly remained. In the words of the old country folks around here, "Making the most of what you have is the best thing to do anyway." That certainly proved to be the case in this situation.

When the rains finally subsided and the slick clay dried out slightly, Preston and his crew, which now consisted of not just the junk man but also a young boy named James, came to attempt to move the ugly little house up to the top of the hill. After the house was in the approximate space we had picked out, the conversation and planning for the foundation and the direction we wanted the house to face took quite a while. It was decided that the front porch would face the western sky so that we might enjoy the afternoon sunsets, and the back of the house would then of course give us a great view of the morning sunrises.

The next step was to bring several loads of railroad crossties to the site so that we could elevate the house a few feet at a time. This was accomplished by having the same "junk guy" with those junk wreckers and the yellow school bus jack the house up with great care, moving upward at such a slow pace the human eye had difficulty seeing it. And at the same time, Prescott and James very cautiously stacked the crossties in square supports under the house. The wrecker pulled a side of the house a little, and at the same time the men under the house kept placing the crossties to that level, then the same procedure took place in another section of the house. Miraculously no one was injured. After repeating this drill several times on the front and back, the ugly little house eventually sat about eight feet in the air. I must say that it looked much better with the elevation, even though it had a long way to go to become even moderately attractive.

The concrete blocks that would form the permanent foundation were not your ordinary concrete blocks, but were oversized and much stronger. The plan was to make a two-car garage with double doors underneath the house, forming a foundation as well providing a workshop for Glenn. When these blocks were all in place, a generous space would run along the top of them in two parallel sections from the front of the building to the back section. Two steel beams placed in these slots would add extra strength so that when the house was finally brought to rest on top of this foundation, there would be no question about the concrete garage holding the house in place.

About this time something rather strange happened. Glenn and Prescott had had a difference of opinion on more than one occasion about details and plans for the next steps. The main difference arose from the fact that Glenn wanted to move a good bit faster, and Prescott wanted to continue to perfect every move at a slower pace. After several afternoons of discussions, Glenn decided that he would just hold off on the rest of the building for the time being and let the dust settle, figuratively and realistically. He explained to Prescott that his bank account was in need of a period of recovery, and a waiting period would be in order for the next few months. Actually the problem was that Prescott had fallen in love with the project and would not listen to any suggestions that did not concur with his plans. It might be said that he had almost forgotten that the house was not his, had lost sight of the ultimate goal, and wanted to complete the project without any input from the owner, Glenn. On the afternoon when Glenn explained the situation to Prescott, an uncanny sadness seemed to fall across the area, and it was as if someone had taken away Prescott's child.

So for several months, nothing happened at the "pig farm." We would go out there from town and look around and wonder what we would do next. Glenn decided that he would try just to complete the garage area so that he would have a place to do workshop stuff, even if he did not finish the house right away. This job could be accomplished by installing a couple of folding garage doors. So the next research project involved finding someone who might be expert enough to install these kinds of doors. We found that because of the unique way the concrete blocks were constructed and the way the steel beams crossed the ceiling of the garage area, installing folding doors that receded into the inner space was almost an impossibility. About this time we met Alton. A casual acquaintance told us that this young man owned some sort of construction business housed in a building with several folding doors—doors that were used to enable the supplies and tools of his trade to be carried in and out as needed.

Our visit to Alton's construction company proved to be the beginning of something more that just acquiring doors: it involved the completion of the house at the pig farm. As we wandered around his rather large compound there, I became aware that this young man had an exceptional talent to use space in a way that was both pleasing and simple. Sort of on the spur of the moment, I asked if he did any small jobs like we needed to have done for the ugly house at the farm and if possibly he could add a spacious room and a bath to the existing country house on the concrete blocks. He agreed to come out and see just how far we had come with the project and what would be needed to do the remainder of the building. Somewhere in all of this, doors were discussed and that problem was solved also.

Alton came out for our meeting and agreed to take on the challenge of completing the construction, adding on one spacious room with a bath, and adding a deck to the rear of the house. We agreed that the new annex needed to conform to the lines of the original house, and so the addition would be placed on poles eight feet high to be at the level of the house placed on the concrete block foundation. In addition, the roofline had to be slanted to match the line of the old house. The finished product was an architect's worst nightmare: on the north side, a concrete block-based old farm house; on the south side, a new addition placed on poles; on the back of these, a large deck with wide steps up to the back door; and a small front porch facing west with only a door to the inside of the house. In other words, there was no way to exit the porch to the outside because the porch rested on the steel beam, which elevated it eight feet above the ground. The saving grace of this dwelling was the abundance of windows, which provided that magnificent view we had worked so hard to obtain. Most of the errors in design were forgiven by the frequent visitors when they came into the house because they were immediately overcome by the light coming from all directions, the view of woods seen through the many windows and the grasping sense of non-conformity radiated by the whole house. However, when we walked into the house, our eyes were not just on the view as it existed at that time, but rather on what more could be done outside to make the view even better.

Before we began working on the property, almost all of the trees had been logged by the original owner, and the only trees of any significance were in the distant tree line of the forest, which surrounded most of the land. Several small chinaberry trees were scattered around in an area near the house, and so we named the place Chinaberry Ranch. Why "ranch"? It was a joke. We had no horses, cows, buffaloes or any other animals, but Glenn reasoned that the word would make the average person ask questions. And, in Glenn's opinion, if the other person doesn't ask questions, you haven't gotten his attention. Therefore, like so much of what we had done and would do could be considered a joke by normal and usual standards, so giving the place such an odd name only confirmed the insanity of our project. The chinaberry tree also provoked lots of conversation because many people did not know much about it. We had to give a short history about the tree to these unknowing folks, a history which went something like this: When this country was being founded, this tree was imported from the Orient to produce shade on the streets of some of the newly built towns and communities, and in the early part of this century, almost every country house had a single chinaberry tree near the front porch to provide shade. Then when landscaping and more formal yards came about, the chinaberry tree almost disappeared from the yards of most homeowners. However, when some slightly older person hears the words "chinaberry tree," he can be instantly transported back to a childhood filled with memories of sitting under the shade of the tree, using the yellowed and foul-smelling berries for his slingshot, or smelling the sweet lilac blooms in spring. As it turns out, Glenn was successful in achieving his purpose when he named his place Chinaberry Ranch because it certainly caused lots of questions to be asked.

Up to this point, the sequence of events had included buying the land, moving a house onto it, restoring the building, adding to it and giving the place a name. All of this happened in about a year. Then it was time to take the big step, moving into the house. And so, on one of the hottest days August can produce, we moved to Chinaberry Ranch, ready for phase two of this adventure.

A Few Facts About Chinaberry Trees

Common name: chinaberry
Botanical name: *Melia azedarach*
Type: tree
Size: to 40 feet tall
Hardiness: Zones 7-10
Origin: Asia
Light: full sun
Soil: almost any well-drained soil
Growth rate: fast

Descriptions: Imported from Asia in the early frontier days of this country to provide shade along city streets, the chinaberry tree later was planted around farmhouses to furnish a dependable source of firewood. Thriving in adverse conditions and growing at a rapid pace are two of the tree's most valuable assets, even though its life span is short. The crown of the tree forms a dense umbrella-like crown made of glossy green tropical-looking leaves on branches supported by what seems like a strong trunk. However, all of the wood in the chinaberry tree is often described as brittle. In spring, the tree sends forth fragrant lilac blossoms, causing the tree to be referred to in Asia as the "Purple Lilac tree." These blooms soon give way to the formation of clusters of small, shiny green balls, which stay on the tree until the fall, when they turn a dull yellow. A few of these withered, foul-smelling balls fall all during the winter, but the rest almost have to be pushed from the branches in the spring when it is time for the lilac blooms to emerge.

So just like Glenn, the chinaberry tree always has something going on, it can survive adverse conditions and it never gives up. The following passage from *Uncle Tom's Cabin* gives another characterization: "The wagon rolled up a weedy gravel walk, under a noble avenue of China trees, whose graceful forms and ever-springing foliage seemed to

be the only things there that neglect could not daunt or alter—
like noble spirits, so deeply rooted in goodness, as to flourish
and grow stronger amid discouragement and decay."

"You Can't Grow Nothing On This Land"

The small house with more windows than walls gave us the chance to look at miles of wide-open stretches of land and a wide expanse of sky that was constantly changing with weather conditions. While standing to admire the view from these windows, we sensed that the land was begging to be used for some productive purpose. After all, we were surrounded by large Mennonite farms on all sides, farms that produced cotton, soybeans, corn and a variety of other vegetable crops. In fact, these Mennonites were known for their expertise in the farming business. They came to our place frequently to see just what we were going to do with this old pig farm, which they had had an interest in and had taken an active part in with the former owner. Their experiences on this hard clay land were far from pleasant, and they did not offer much encouragement to us. I am sure that if they had been able to voice their frank opinion about the place, they would have expressed surprise that we had purchased it in the first place. It was, I'm sure, beyond their wildest comprehension to understand what we could possibly have been thinking when we decided to buy it. If pigs had not found a happy home here, then how could humans possibly think their lives would be pleasant here?

Because I had grown roses and a variety of flowers in my other life, I decided to put in a small group of rose bushes to test the soil and to have those wonderful blooms in the house again. This turned out to be the beginning of a whole new adventure. Because the soil was so packed down by the pig traffic and years of weather-beaten damage to the surface, we knew that when we planted anything, it would be necessary to make a hole with special care in which to put the plant. A tractor-driven auger became our constant companion when planting anything. We would make a deep and wide hole with the auger, much deeper and wider than would seem necessary for the plant, but we realized early on that the density of the clay, the compact nature of the other soil components, and general weather conditions of Chinaberry Ranch dictated that special planting methods be used. When we planted a rose bush, we would not just go the prescribed depth and width that the instructions gave, but we would multiply this times five. Then we would refill the hole partially with some sort of peat moss or other mulching material. This method worked extremely well, and every rose bush loved its happy home.

On a rather beautiful winter afternoon while we were busy making one of these million dollar holes, one of the local Mennonite farmers happened to stop by for a visit. We did not stop to chat, but continued to construct the future rose hole. At some point in this process, the Mennonite shook his head and said, "You can't grow nothing up here in this dirt, except maybe red root." I promptly asked what exactly was red root. He assured me that I would know it when I saw it. This man was absolutely correct about the red root. I soon learned when it was time to weed the garden that it was next to impossible to like. This aggressively growing plant shot up from the soil with a vengeance like nothing I had ever seen, armed with thorns and a long, red carrot-like root, which could hardly be pulled from the dirt. But he was very wrong about growing anything else in this dirt. The following spring the roses were beautiful. They seemed to grow to unusual proportions and had very few diseases. The harvest of blooms was so bountiful, I ended up sharing them with lots of people. We took this abundance as an omen. We now had the incentive to plant, and we knew that if roses did so well, it should be fairly easy to grow other things.

Looking back to the beginning of this place, it now seems funny that the land appeared to beckon to us and almost demanded to be used for a worthwhile purpose. I am reminded each time I reflect about the evolution of this place that our journeys in life are not exactly laid out in an orderly fashion, but rather we inch along with blind faith as if we are stepping from stone to stone in a fast-moving stream, just trying to reach the other side with the least amount of trouble or danger. After much discussion, we could not decide what to grow on all this land, but we did know that we wanted to grow something. We came to the conclusion that we did not want to grow the usual corn, soybeans, cotton and other crops. We were trying to find something that would be interesting and fun to grow. So before this was a flower farm, it was a bamboo ranch. Why bamboo? Because we read an article about all the new products that were being made from this ancient plant. In the 1990s, there was an abundance of print material about the bamboo industry. It was described as the wood of the future. The more research we did, the more interested we became, not just in the bamboo of today, but also in the history of it. We, like everyone else, had heard that old saying about bamboo—that "it will take over"—and that is about all we knew starting out. Maybe subconsciously we hoped bamboo or something would take over, because being surrounded with all that bare ground made us anxious to get something growing.

Fate moved in to tempt us further when in 1995, the National Bamboo Convention was held in Savannah, Georgia, only about a two-hour drive from our farm. We thought this occurrence was too good to be true. There was not much time between deciding to go and finishing our research on the subject. We were fast stuffing our brains with all of the available literature and asking all the questions we could possibly think of in order to prepare ourselves for the convention. When we arrived in Savannah, we were not prepared for the diversity of the crowd or the diversity of the bamboo plant itself.

We soon learned that this particular place, named the Coastal Gardens Historic Bamboo & Horticultural Collection, had been around for a very long time, and that it had been the direct source from which most of the bamboo was shipped in this country in the early part of the century. This conference sponsored by the American Bamboo Society, or the ABS, had drawn attendees from all over the United States and some other parts of the world. It was not a large crowd, but it certainly was the most diverse group I had ever seen. All of the participants, no matter their origin, were extremely enthusiastic about bamboo and seemed to have a great deal of information about it. We felt like rank amateurs for most of the time we were there, but because we listened and asked lots of questions, we learned about bamboo, and we learned to appreciate its value almost instantly. We changed from the usual normal people who subscribed to the old theory that "bamboo will take over" to the quintessential enthusiasts who could give the man on the street several reasons to love bamboo.

These bamboo farmers who came from all over were busy passing out their business cards, which stated their particular involvement with bamboo and how they were turning this plant into a money-making project. Some farmers were making and installing bamboo fences, some made lumber for floors and building houses, a small group had brought their artistic products, and some just passed out plant catalogs to encourage others to order plants through them. It was impossible to be among this group of fanatics and not consider bamboo somewhat of a miracle plant. The following excerpt is from the ABS brochure:

"The thought of bamboo often conjures up a number of images: oriental landscapes, lush tropics, baskets, crafts, musical instruments, fishing poles, and the giant panda.

Although it is grown in this country primarily for landscaping, bamboo has been, and yet remains, one of the single most important plants to the largest number of people in the world. Bamboo has found its way into folklore, rituals, sports, construction, the arts and music, the kitchen, as well as the garden.

The Chinese used bamboo for constructing gas lines in 1000 BC.

Thomas Edison used a bamboo filament in his light bulb experiment.

A bamboo suspension bridge (the largest of its kind—over 250 yards long) crosses the River Min in China.

Bamboo is a member of the grass family *Gramineae (Poaceae)*, with over 50 genera and over 1.230 documented species and varieties. It is native on all continents except Europe and Antarctica.

Bamboo may be found at altitudes from sea level up to almost 10,000 feet; it tolerates a range of temperatures from tropical to the very cold-tolerant Himalayan Mountain bamboos that survive temperatures as low as minus 20 degrees F.

Over one million tons of bamboo is harvested annually worldwide—enough board feet to cover over 200 times the circumference of the earth—for construction use.

Deforestation and habitat destruction by human populations are threatening native strands of bamboos, and the animals dependent on them, throughout the world.

Bamboos are among the most primitive grasses, surviving on this planet between one and two hundred million years (200 to 400 times as long as the total lifetime of the human race).

Like a grass unlike a tree, bamboo sends up its new

shoots to reach its full height in one year's growth. It may grow as much as 100 feet in the tropics with a diameter of more than a foot, in one month's time.

In today's gardens, grasses are very popular, and bamboo is certainly the "king" of the grasses. Many varieties are suitable for container gardening, and bamboo is finding still another niche in this country as bonsai.

With variations in growth, habits, culm color and shape, variegation of leaves, etc., it is easy to see why bamboo is grown in this country as an element in the landscape....as a stately forest, elegant specimen or shade-loving ground cover."

CB❧

AFTER A COUPLE of days with these bamboo experts, we were beginning to get the fever as we visited with them and attended slide shows accompanied by scintillating speeches. The grounds of the Coastal Gardens were divided into many square plots where different varieties of bamboo were growing and being cultivated for the purposes of perpetuation, sales, and distribution. Out in these square plots we were given demonstrations of how to cultivate bamboo and how to dig up a plant, and general information about the growing of bamboo. We were told about a special shovel, which they happened to sell, that could properly dig straight down in the soil to remove a rhizome. A rhizome is the horizontal underground root system of the bamboo plant, the place where shoots are sent out from nodules to sprout above ground and allow the plant to spread. Because this growth takes place out of sight, the plant has the reputation of "taking over." Anyone who has ever had the experience of digging up a bamboo rhizome understands why the plant is allowed to grow independently anywhere it chooses. Not only does it require a great deal of strength to get to the root system, but also separating the underground stem from the remainder of the plant is somewhat of a Samsonian endeavor. It was at this juncture that we were deciding that maybe we did not want to have a bamboo farm after all.

The final night of the American Bamboo Society conference was capped off with an auction of certain kinds of potted bamboo plants. The people handling the details also gave a single door prize, which was something called a "tiny fern" bamboo. The plant was brought out to allow everyone to have a look before the magic number was drawn. As the plant was brought out, I remarked to Glenn, "Gosh! I would love to have that plant." It had frilly and dainty curved branches with very small leaves, which did indeed make it resemble some kind of fern. When the number was drawn, would you believe it was my number? The lady sitting directly behind me leaned over my left shoulder and inquired, "Lady, do you always get everything you wish for??" I assured her that this was a once-in-a-lifetime occurrence, and that bamboo must have some sort of magic attached to it for me to win the plant. Glenn must have just gotten the magic bamboo fever because before the auction was over, he had purchased three different varieties.

We left Savannah the next day with the car loaded with the door prize bamboo and the three specimens we had purchased. It took a lot of talent to get that much bamboo into our car, but we finally took off with the branches protruding out every window and with us crowded into as small a space as possible. About halfway home, I would have sworn that the old saying was true, the one about bamboo "taking over," because it seemed that the plants were beginning to multiply in that small car. After about two hours of bamboo rubbing, we arrived back at the ugly "pig farm," unloaded the plants, and sat down to ponder whether we really wanted to be in the bamboo business.

The next day we picked out some places to set out the new plants, and we set about digging those special holes in which to plant them. On each of the plants was a metal tag with the botanical name. We had one *phyllostacys heterocycla pubescens*, one *pleioblastus gramineus*, and one *phyllostachys nidularia farcta*. In addition to these three varieties, we had the "tiny fern" whose botanical name was never clearly defined. When we backed away to admire our purchases and the door prize, we did not express any desire to go further with the bamboo business. We had learned from these bamboo experts about the difficulty of growing, harvesting and especially marketing this plant. However, we did make one more purchase after that. We were called by one of those enthusiasts we had met in Savannah to inquire if we would be interested in obtaining some unusual black bamboo. He further explained that there was an ongoing project to rid a certain area near his hometown of the black bamboo forest, and therefore the owners were giving away the plants if you were willing to dig them up yourselves. I guess we still had enough of the bamboo fever to go right away and start digging. That is exactly what we did. We took our newly purchased bamboo shovel and a small trailer and away we went. We dug and dug and dug. We headed home with the small trailer loaded with four or five fine black bamboo plants. At least on this trip we were not crowded out of the car by the plants and consequently felt more kindly toward them on arrival. We decided to plant all these specimens in a small grove by themselves in the front of the house. This special place for the black bamboo has turned out to be perfect because we enjoy seeing them swaying in the breeze with their dramatic black stalks casting a beautiful picture of contrast against the sky and other trees.

So that was the end of the bamboo adventure, as far as a business is concerned. But nearly every day at some point, we still stop to admire what is going on with the plants. Believe me, there is always something going on. The way wind moves through bamboo is lovely, the different way each kind of plant grows is interesting, and whether above ground or below ground, the plant is always doing something. But my attraction to the bamboo plant is more than this. I think I have decided that if we humans could be more "bamboo-like," it would be a good thing. That swaying with the breeze rather than standing stiff in defiance would make us stronger in the face of adversity. That strong root system, giving rise to new beginnings, would give us a strong base from which to grow. That individual beauty that would set us apart from others would let us know that it is all right to be different. Bamboo watching is a great soothing pastime. I am glad we did not get in the bamboo business because I am not sure we could have taken the time to enjoy exactly what the plant is all about.

From Buckeye Bamboo Company To Chinaberry Ranch Flower Farm

The rose bushes had grown to such glory that it seemed only a natural move to the planting of other kinds of flowers, and especially since I had had some friends ask if I might make a few flower arrangements for them on special occasions. Of course Fate was doing her little trick again where, as a player, you are unaware that a simple little arrangement made with spectacular flowers could lead to something entirely in another realm. Flowers speak to people in different languages and affect each of us in a special and meaningful way. A simple arrangement set in the middle of a small dinner table can give a different message to each person seated around the table. Flowers not only present themselves for viewing, but they also provoke memories of childhood or previous gala occasions as well as decorate the settings in which they are placed. It need not be an elaborate arrangement to induce a precious memory. It can be just a single flower in a bud vase.

The idea that we might get into the cut flower business happened quite by accident as a result of one of these small dinner parties. We had furnished the flowers for the party and were also included in the guest list. Upon arriving at the home of our host and hostess, I was greeted by a local businessman who was very excited about the arrangement of cosmos I had made. He explained that he had not seen cosmos since he was a small child and that his mother had grown them in their garden. I was surprised for a number of reasons. First of all, I had no background in this area because I grew up without flower gardens. There were always vegetable gardens, but no flower gardens. Where I came from on the socioeconomic scale, flowers were a luxury item well beyond our means. Secondly, I was amazed that this was a man, a businessman at that, who appreciated the beauty of fresh flowers. I had always thought that flowers were a woman thing. I was further surprised later when I learned that this businessman owned and operated a funeral home. My thought about this situation was that this man sees thousands of different kinds of flowers on almost a daily basis, yet he was impressed with the common little cosmos. How interesting! Once again I was startled by the view from someone else's soul and how the programming that goes into each of us is dictated by the paths we travel to get where we are going.

For days after returning home from the party, I was unable to get the picture of this rather stodgy businessman and his appreciation of the cosmos out of my mind. I kept thinking that there could not be a better gift than that of growing simple flowers in our fields for others to enjoy. Flowers like cosmos, zinnias, sunflowers, butterfly weed, veronica, and Queen Anne's lace were just some of the varieties that came to mind in the beginning. So with all this unused land, except for where the bamboo plants were, and a mind running wild with flower plans, we started to make flowerbeds out of what had been pig-feeding pads.

As I mentioned in the beginning when describing this ugly piece of property, there were several long and badly made concrete sections around the barn and house, placed in no particular pattern. Just as a matter of reference, we started to call these concrete atrocities "pig feeding pads," which is what we thought the pig farmer might have used them for, but we were just going on pure assumption. It was of no particular interest to me to find out what their original purpose was, but I was vitally interested in finding a way to disguise them. It wasn't bad enough that they were there, but they were also above ground level. Over the years, the dirt had eroded from them, leaving the jagged edges to call attention to an already unattractive sight. In retrospect, I am not sure I was interested in growing flowers; maybe it was in an effort to hide these awful concrete pads that I came up with the idea of making the ground that surrounded them into a bed.

One day while assessing this situation and looking around for a solution, my eyes came upon a rather large stack of railroad crossties purchased for the construction of the house. Once the house had been elevated and put in its permanent position, the crossties were left there with no particular purpose. Right away the idea came to me that a solution to the eroded edges of the concrete pads would be to place the extra crossties around them and fill in with soil to make large flowerbeds. Because of the erosion problem on this property, crossties were the perfect answer to preventing the heavy rains from washing away the prepared soil. With Herculean effort, Glenn moved into place each of the creosoted crossties, forming a surrounding wall for the concrete pads. Once these were in place and the dirt was added, the place looked much better, even without the flowers being there. Of course, with this lovely, rich dirt all in place and ready for planting, I could hardly wait to get those seeds in there and have the big bloom happen. For those of us who have a love affair with dirt, there is hardly a greater thrill than the sight of weeded, dark, rich, perfectly tilled soil. There is a magnetism and expectancy about what the earth can bring forth from this granular collection of dirt when a human adds a little work and caring to it. The partnership of dirt and the worker of it is like no other. Therefore, it is not surprising that gardening is widely held as a great therapy for the disturbed because having this relationship is all about giving and getting back. The combination of sharing and caring is all there is to growing. Whether growing flowers, vegetables, row crops, or trees, it is all about the farmer giving time and effort to the earth and the earth giving back the product many fold.

With the beds properly made and the seeds placed carefully in them with fertilizer and mulch, the waiting period began. We were pretty sure that the flowers would do well, given what our experience had been with the rose bushes, but we were still anxious to see what would happen. As the last cool days of winter melted into the warmer days of spring, we had our first excitement when the tiny seedlings began to stick their heads through the soil. Zinnias, sunflowers, celosia, butterfly weed, Mexican sunflower, cosmos, rosemary, and lavender were some of the seeds and plants we placed in the newly constructed pig pad beds. When dealing with seed, there is a certain magic that is unexplained and the development of this little, dry and seemingly dead parcel is truly a miracle of sorts, particularly since all of this coming to life takes place under the earth in secret. Having said that gardening is about sharing and caring, I must now add faith. From the beginning of the process, I guess there is a sprinkling of faith throughout because without faith, no one would till the soil, prepare the bed or plant the seed. Faith is taken to another level when the grower has to wait patiently for the seed to develop and become life. I am tempted sometime to say, when asked about having a "green thumb," that the missing element in most failed gardeners could possibly be this faith component. I am sure that if flowers could talk, they would suggest faith in them as the most necessary of all things. After all, if other people do not have faith in us, how well do we as humans function?

The "pig pads" proved to be the best of all flowerbeds. They produced thousands of blooms. Because I became so caught up in the production of flowers, I failed to research the market end of the business. So there we were with all of the flowers blooming their heads off in the field and no one to use them. I had to make the rounds in the surrounding little communities to ask if some florists might use them in their businesses. This was truly a difficult endeavor because all small florists in this rural region had used the same old glads, non-fragrant roses, and rubber fern for years and had little time to be educated in the new trend toward the simple flowers of yesterday. In a few words, there was not a market except for the small group of people who knew about our flowers from the "dinner party" circuit. But then, there isn't a downside to having too many flowers because we had our house full of them most of time, and we gave away so many that our generosity became a form of marketing and public relations without our even realizing it. All the while we were establishing a reputation for having these unusual and beautiful flowers that seemed to have a long vase life and fragrance.

Finally, I realized that the more I put those flowers out there for the public to see, the better our chances for us to create a market for them. Just such an occasion arose one summer day. On a Sunday afternoon, the nearby small town was to have a grand opening of its new library, of which it was extremely proud. I called the powers that be and asked if they would like for me to bring several flower arrangements to this opening to help with the festivities. They were excited and appreciative, especially since their budget did not allow for this type of luxury. The Saturday before the big day, I was busy cutting and conditioning the flowers, getting containers washed and ready, not to mention wondering just how I would transport these eight or ten arrangements into town. But I just kept busy with the flowers, knowing that somehow it would work out. While in this busy mode, I began to reflect about my first attempt at a flower arrangement. I often reflected in this way because doing so offered me a bittersweet mixture of pleasure and pain and reminded me that sometimes the

Fate monster is at work when you least expect it.

My first attempt at placing cut flowers in a container for the purpose of decoration or whatever happened quite by accident. As I said, I was reared in a family without cut flowers in the yard or house, and our closest association with flowers came at funerals and weddings. When I was in college, my boyfriend and I were invited to a party at his roommate's house located in a part of the state that was known for its vast estates, hunting plantations and horse farms. Upon arriving at our destination—a house resembling a mansion, featuring many acres with grazing horses and gardens filled with flowers of every description—I immediately knew I was in a social setting with which I was unfamiliar. We entered the front foyer of the huge house and were greeted warmly by the roommate coming in from the back part of the building. While we were standing there having a nice little chat, the French doors that led from the terrace to the library were swung open with a flourish, and a lovely older lady, carrying a straw flower basket filled to the brim with exquisite blooms, came gliding into the room. Only in magazines had I seen any other woman who looked like her—adorned in a large-brimmed gardening hat, the casual but fashionable attire of the wealthy, and having the confident air of being completely comfortable with her affluent surroundings. This was the roommate's mother, and he promptly introduced her to us. Without wasting much time, she turned to me and asked if I would take the flowers and arrange them in the cut glass vase on the grand piano in the library. She did not wait for me to answer her but handed me the basket and the clippers as she fled up the winding staircase to the second floor. Almost as soon as she had disappeared, the boys left for the terrace, and I was there all alone with the flowers and the scary task of arranging them in that vase. To comprehend my extreme degree of fear, it is necessary to understand that I had never before held a fresh cut flower or seen a cut glass vase. Putting the two luxury items together in any sort of display seemed like a little more than impossible.

After looking around for some kind of help and assistance, and realizing none was available, I took a deep breath and moved to the vase on the piano. I set the basket on the floor, put the clippers in my right hand and decided that this could not be that difficult for one reason. It was an epiphany that has stayed with me through the years as I have continued from that day forward to do flower arrangements for myself and other people. The bright deduction that came to my mind that day was the fact that if you have beautiful fresh flowers and a container that complements them, nothing else is necessary. I began to clip a few ends off the flowers, placing them in the vase in a rather nonchalant fashion, and as I repeated this process, I became rather comfortable with the whole situation. Backing away to observe the arrangement, I sensed that it did not look too bad for a beginner. However, I did know that when the lady of the house came in, she might have an entirely different opinion. Just as these moments of doubt were crowding in on me, she appeared at the door of the room, uttering complimentary remarks as she moved toward the piano and the arrangement. Trial by fire is not always a bad thing. In fact, since that day, I have had very little trouble making flower arrangements, no matter what the circumstances.

I was jerked back to consciousness when I realized that there was not much time until the opening of the library the next day. So I set about to get the containers filled with all the different blooms we had grown at this pig farm, fully appreciating that the patrons at the opening would know that these flowers were not the normal variety from the local florist. Upon completing the task, I remembered that I had no way to transport this number of arrangements because at that time, we did not own a van or a vehicle large enough to carry them. I called a local lady who suggested that I call Gerry.

Gerry:
The Cosmos Man

S ome people are just "too nice" for this world. Gerry was
one of those, one who always had a kind word that soothed
the spirit, a slight and genuine smile that brightened the soul,
and a nature so serene that you just knew everything would
be all right. What a marvelous personality for someone who
cared for the family and loved ones of the dead and dying.
You see, Gerry was the owner of a funeral home in a small
town, where all the townsfolk wanted him to take special care
of them at their desperate time of need, and they wanted him
personally to take care of them. One of his assistants would
not do in such cases, and so he labored long hours and under
extreme circumstances in many tedious situations. In these
small towns, the funeral director or owner of the funeral home
is counted on not only for all the preparations and legalities
having to do with the dead, but also for administering to the
family and friends on a personal level. Gerry was a natural
at carrying out this duty because his father before him had
been in this same business, and he had grown up knowing
just what to say and how to calm a soul loaded with sorrow
at the time of the death of a family member or friend.

Huge mounds of brightly colored flowers, ornate baskets

loaded with every variety of flowers, different pots of live plants, short-stemmed white buds made in the shape of hearts and crosses—all of these kinds of flowers Gerry saw and worked with on almost a daily basis. However, this enormous array of floral arrangements did not dull his appreciation of flowers and the special need they fill because he understood so clearly the sorrow and pain of his clients. Most of us have to make a slight adjustment in our thinking to understand another's problem. Not so with Gerry. He could just know how to understand in the subtlest of ways. When his kind eyes saw pain or problems, he just very patiently responded in a quiet and caring fashion.

I first became aware of this kind and problem-solving man when I needed to transport my flower arrangements from our farm to the opening of the new library in town. Because Chinaberry Ranch is about twelve miles from town and at that time, we did not have our own van, a friend suggested that Gerry would be glad for us to borrow one of his funeral flower vans for the Sunday afternoon celebration. So our needs were not about a death or anything so important, but Gerry managed the situation with the same kind of interest and cooperation. He was eager to lend us the vehicle, allowed us to keep it over the weekend and offered to pick it up on the following day. Some politicians and "do-gooders" strive to have their names engraved on those plaques that hang just inside libraries and other public buildings, but Gerry and others like him strive to make life easier for the rest of us and never expect or want to hear much about gratitude. In fact, Gerry seemed almost embarrassed by any form of credit or publicity. If the truth were known, I think on the Sunday afternoon that the library had its big opening, Gerry just knew that those flowers would help the visitors enjoy their new facility in a better way. So he did us a big favor and made the opening a grander affair while he stayed quietly in the background with that slight smile on his face.

Even in a social setting, he had a certain kindness the rest of us do not possess. Frequently at dinner parties, the conversation would turn to some small town gossip that does seem to help entertain all of us when the food and drink is served. On more than one of these evenings, I noticed that Gerry never had an unkind word to say about anyone and would even add some comment that gave a better slant to the subject or made the person being discussed seem nicer. It is a rare talent to be able to enjoy the company of friends in this setting and still maintain some dignity without being perceived as a stick-in-the-mud. Gerry could do this with so much grace and charm that his uniqueness often went unnoticed, hidden behind his quiet and kind nature.

So for many years Gerry watched from his funeral home as people in the small town lived and died. He cared for all their needs as if they were members of his own family. And then on a rainy autumn Monday, Gerry took his own life, and the town mourned in a way that they were not accustomed to. After all, the person who had helped them with their suffering and grief was gone. All the memories of the kind smile, the quiet nature and the unassuming manner flooded back in the minds of the people of the small town. How could he do this? After all, he was their expert in the art of dying and how to cope with it. Most of us are afraid of death. He was not. I like to think that Gerry was expert in managing death and almost thought of it as an old acquaintance. It was life that he could not handle. Some people are just "too nice" for this world. He was one of those.

And so when I look in the face of a beautiful, delicate cosmos, I always think of Gerry because he told me at that dinner party about his mother growing them when he was a child. But also I think of him because the cosmos is gentle, delicate and unable to withstand much pain. Cosmos are almost too nice for this world—just like Gerry.

A Few Facts About Cosmos

Common name: cosmos
Botanical name: *Cosmos bipinnatus*
Type: reseeding annual
Size: 3-6 feet tall
Origin: Mexico
Light: full sun
Soil: well-drained
Growth rate: moderate
Description: The name *cosmos* comes from a Greek word meaning "beautiful" and does not refer to asteroids, comets, or anything celestial. The main image the flower evokes is one of old-fashioned cottage gardens filled with silky blossoms of red, pink, lavender, rose and white supported by slender stems with delicate filigreed leaves. The plant has a tendency to flop, making it less than desirable for gardeners who like tidy and formal rows of flowers in their beds.

Just like Gerry, Chess McKinney loved cosmos. She wrote in *Memories of Grandmother's Garden*, "How pretty to this child's mind were the handful of brilliant cosmos stuck in a glass container, nothing could be more lovely than Granny's bouquet of cosmos."

ೞ

THE LIBRARY FLOWER show with the pig farm flowers was a great success. Even today I run into people who remember the flowers from that opening.

ೞ

WHILE WE WERE attending the library opening, I spotted the glamorous Harriett.

Harriett:
The Sunflower Lady

A term used to describe both Harriett and the sunflower is "in charge." Just as a garden is ruled by the presence of a few sunflowers, Harriett took charge in the gardens of her life. Before meeting and getting to know her, I had never paid much attention to how certain people make particular flowers their own personal favorites. Everything has a pattern in life, and it certainly holds true with people and flowers now that I have stopped and thought about it. It isn't just an accident that someone like Harriett would select the sunflower as her preferred flower. Their personalities are perfectly matched.

The first time I saw Harriett, she came hastily striding through an office where I worked as a front desk person. Her very presence in a room filled any space not already taken, not in a bad way, but one might say in an abundant way. She had the unique ability to just step into the room and have it react to her presence. When some people walk into a perfectly empty room, there is no change in the atmosphere of the room. These same types of people can make a statement or make a loud noise, and there is still an emptiness there. However, someone with Harriett's personality can fill space with grace and striking, bold nuances. She did not have to say anything or make any move. All she had to do was step into the room, and right away things changed.

When I looked up from my desk, she was moving with purpose through the small office like her mission was of the utmost importance. This was the American Cancer Society office, and her purpose was a volunteer endeavor, not a business situation. Her very dark hair was neatly coiffured, her small-framed body was perfectly clothed, her face was tastefully made up, and her manner was extremely polite. But her mission was to accomplish her task and move on—she was in charge. No time was wasted with idle chatter or palaver. Whatever paperwork, schedule of events or appointments she needed to discuss with the director was taken care of in just a few minutes, and then she moved out the back door to her car so she could make the next appointment or luncheon, or whatever her game plan called for.

After she left the office, there was a certain emptiness that had not been there before she came. Just as she filled the empty spaces when she came into the room, when she left, an even greater void was felt. When I returned to my desk, I just sat for a few minutes thinking about Harriett and wondering about this kind of person who exudes this mix of boldness and striking nuances and yet gives off the favorable essence of compatibility in almost every situation. I wondered whether this was a talent learned or a special gift from birth.

Some time later, I began seeing Harriett's picture in the local newspaper and noticing her in appearances on the local television station. Of course, she had been doing this type of thing for a long time. It was I who had just come to town and started to observe her and her town. I would see a picture of her at a church benefit, or with the Daughters of the American Revolution, or at a school function, and the list went on and on. It was not unusual to see her on television with a panel discussing poetry, or local politics or fund-raising. Even though I had no reason to come in close contact with her, she just exuded that certain charisma that made me want to know more about her. It would be a few years before I would personally get to know this woman and fully appreciate what kind of unusual personality she possessed.

As time went by, I did begin to have some contact with Harriett at local functions and social gatherings around our small town. This was due in part to the sharing of certain mutual friends and to my newcomer status, which provoked certain questions from her, as is the case with most Harrietts of the world. One of the intriguing things about people with her personality type is that they always seem to be vitally interested in other people. She happened to be at one of those dinner parties where my flowers were on display, and she was most complimentary about them. She sought me out of the crowd and questioned me about the flower farm. Surprised at the location of the farm, she launched into a detailed account of just how that particular part of the county had years ago been the best and largest farm area anywhere around. She further explained that the large landowner had enjoyed bountiful crop productions of all kinds because the land was so very fertile. This was the first time that Glenn and I had ever heard any kind words about the "dirt" we had been trying to till against all odds according the present-day inhabitants. This news was like suddenly hearing about the previous life of someone you had formerly know only in his or her present state. It seemed reasonable for us to think that if the land had been fertile years ago, we could make it produce again. I asked what had happened to the large landowners and their farms, and Harriett explained that many years ago there was some sort of sickness associated with the area causing the families to move away. This news did not dampen our enthusiasm in any way because we had already grown to think of the place as a transformation project extraordinaire, sort of a Pygmalion-type thing. (Maybe that should be spelled Pigmalion in honor of the pigs that lived there before we did!)

Soon after this encounter, Harriett began calling me for flowers. If she were having her garden club, she would telephone to place an order for whatever I had blooming at the time, yet she almost always mentioned to me that she preferred sunflowers. Even though she would take any kind of simple garden flowers, she would usually remind me that she was not particularly fond of roses. Her adamancy about this flower always shocked me a little, particularly since the rose is my personal favorite and was probably what made me stop and realize that the kinds of flowers people prefer do have connections to their personalities. If she were having a bridal shower, she would express the same preference about the sunflowers or simple flowers. The occasion seemed to have little to do with the appropriateness of the flower. Her statement was that the sunflower was part of her persona, and since she was the hostess, that should be the flower for any special celebration. I never had to make arrangements for Harriett. She would tell me to leave the flowers on her back porch, and she would fix them in her containers and to her satisfaction. I loved this idea because I could almost picture her enjoying handling the flowers in a special way and making the arrangement an expression of what she was all about. This flower exchange worked very well for both of us. There was no meeting between the two of us at a certain time, no exchange of money at the scene, no worry about returning my containers. She had a plan that was simple and most efficient—just like the rest of her agenda. I would leave the flowers with a bill placed underneath them on her back steps, and she would take them inside at her convenience, placing the empty containers on her washing machine in the utility room adjacent to the back steps. The next day I would receive a check in the mail, without fail, and the next time I went into town, I would pick up the empty containers. This method worked so well after a while that all she had to do was call and simply say, "Robbie, I need some flowers," and we both knew the drill from that point on.

And then there were the times I would drive into town for groceries or to run other errands, and I would see a lady striding along the sidewalks at a rather fast clip, head down, seemingly moving toward an important goal of some kind. She did not amble, saunter, or stroll. She was on a mission. It was only after I had seen her several times that I realized that it was Harriett. She never waved to passersby, nor did I ever see her engaged in a friendly chat when she was out for her walk. I happen to think a great deal can be learned about a person by the way he walks. If a person moves at a slow, leisurely pace, it is probably because it reflects his personality and his sense of timing in other endeavors, not just in walking. If a person walks too fast, there is reason to think that he might not be concerned with small details and does not mind missing out on something. But the way Harriett walked those times I saw her told me that her walk was like a sunflower would walk if it could. In fact, her walk was not the only thing about her that reminded me of a sunflower. Her strong will, her love of bright colors, her attention to detail and her mission to help other people were just some of the traits that made her sunflower-like. This flower demands attention in the garden, but it isn't just for show. On close observation, it is easy to see that the flower is more complex and has more meaning than just its strong demanding appearance. I had never paid much attention to the center of the sunflower until I started to raise sunflowers commercially and had the opportunity to watch the changes in the seedpod at the center. This is constantly changing every day after the flower opens wide and continues to change until it is ripe, becoming a much sought-after food. The combination of beauty and worthwhileness is the best of all worlds.

Upon learning that Harriett had been a schoolteacher for many years, I immediately pictured the unique and enviable position her students must have enjoyed. Having someone like Harriett standing in front of the classroom, offering informative instruction and giving direction from her well of intelligence and experience, would give the average student unlimited advantages. Harriett told me the following interesting story about one of her teaching positions at a small college in Georgia:

It was the custom at this small college to have a pair of teachers be in charge of the social functions during the school year. The two teachers had to be responsible for the food and decoration for whatever the function during the time of year that it was to take place. She and her teacher partner, John, drew the fall season when the year's plans were decided, and they were not at all happy because decorating seemed more difficult for this season. In addition, they were not happy about spending their own money for these expenses, which had become the custom of the college. Harriett decided to make a visit to the president of the college to ask him for some funding for the social function in order to make their difficult task somewhat easier. She did not get her funds. She was informed that the school was running short of money and the expenses would have to be shouldered by her and her partner. After much discussion, they came upon the idea of using fall foliage as the primary decoration for the auditorium, thereby defraying some expense and keeping the seasonal theme intact.

John arrived on the campus one brisk fall morning with the news that on the way in from his drive to work, he had passed a grove of trees with the most beautifully colored branches and wondered if they might use them for their decorations. Harriett asked what kind of trees these might be, but John said that he wasn't sure. They decided that they would use the branches anyway, and a plan was made for John to bring them in on the appointed day.

On the day of the event, Harriett was waiting outside the auditorium when John arrived with a car loaded to the roof with these brightly colored branches. When she looked inside the car, she was a little dismayed because the car was filled with chinaberry leaves. She was very familiar with these leaves and the tree from which they had come, because like most Southerners, she had grown up with at least one of these trees in her yard. Memories came flooding back of the slingshots loaded with the hard berries from these trees, the unpleasant scent from the berries when they were mashed underfoot and the pleasant lilac scent of the purple blooms in the spring. As a young child Harriett especially loved the rather large branching trunk of the tree because it afforded her a quick climb when her mother wanted her to do some undesirable task around the house. She climbed up the chinaberry tree and hid among the thick foliage, leaving her mother calling from the back door with little knowledge of her whereabouts. When Harriett was brought back to the present, she saw John was standing by his car with a look of befuddlement on his face, not realizing why she had reacted strangely to his cargo. Harriett decided that it would be better not to explain her mixed feelings about the leaves to John because he might not understand her confusion and reluctance about using them for decorations. The commonality of this tree in the South might make the special speaker feel a little less special if he knew the tree as well as Harriett did, but there was the outside chance that the speaker would not be familiar with this common Southern tree. He might be like John and just think that it was something beautiful and unusual. Anyway time did not permit them to change their decorating plans, and so they set about to place the yellow branches around the stage in the most elaborate fashion.

When it was time for the special speaker to come to the podium, everyone in the audience was aware of the big smile on the speaker's face, a famous face and an even more famous smile. As he began his speech, the smile broke into an audible laugh. He said, "I have spoken all over the country, banked by exotic orchids, beautiful displays of roses, gigantic ferns and luscious greenery, but never have I been blanketed by chinaberry leaves before!" The Honorable Jimmy Carter knew more about chinaberry leaves than even Harriett or the rest of the audience. He probably felt right at home nestled in among these familiar branches since he had grown up in Southwest Georgia.

When I look in the face of the sunflower, I always think of Harriett. There was the day she called me and requested her usual flowers, and I could tell that her voice carried a small amount of sadness and grief. It was our usual custom to arrive at a bouquet size by her telling me where she might be putting the flowers. So I inquired about the room in her house in which she would be using the flowers, and what might be the occasion for which she needed them. Her reply was peppered with the same depressed tone, which told me volumes about her. She said, "There is no special occasion. I just need a few flowers for my soul." I then realized that even "sunflower people," who appear to be strong and in charge, have bad days or low moments like the rest of us.

A Few Facts About Sunflowers

Common name: sunflower
Botanical name: *Helianthus annuus*
Type: annual mainly with few perennial types

Soil: any well-drained soil with heavy fertilizer
Light: full sun
Size: 2-10 ft. tall
Description: The flower is spectacular in the garden whether it is a single plant or a whole field of them because of the bright color, tall stems and unyielding display of strength. It is not only a decorative gardener's delight, but is also an agricultural money-maker with its leaves being used for fodder and its flowers producing a yellow dye. The seeds also contain oil and are used for food.

So when I see a beautiful, robust sunflower standing tall and in my face, I always think of Harriett because the colors are striking, the edges are so very emphatic, and I just know that there has to be a message of hope within the dark center where the seeds will form. Not many people and few plants can be lovely and useful, but the combination is alive and well in Harriett and the sunflower.

Helen And W.L.:
The Iceland Poppy People

W.L. was a hairdresser before male hairdressers were all the rage, a long time ago, when it took a lot of nerve to be in that profession if you were male. Of course, Helen was there at his side doing everything within her power and grasp to help. Back then, there were male barbers, but most of the hairdressers were women, and that was just the way things were. These were a few of the facts that I learned about this couple after getting to know them on a personal basis and establishing a great friendship with them. Remember, I was "not from around here," so I had to learn about W.L. and Helen, as well as lots of other nice people, by being in the area for a while.

For a short time, when I first came to Dublin, I leased a small cottage-type house that was located near the home of W.L. and Helen. At that time the only thing I knew about them was their house—an outstanding tribute to the properly cleaned window and the picture-perfect yard, and the closest thing to outstandingly perfect all-around that I had ever seen—though I had never been inside it. I found that every time I drove past their house, I almost had to stop because the windows were that brilliant, the yard was that immaculate, and the house radiated some sort of "Look at me—these people take very good care of me" message. All the time that I was admiring this place and wondering who could make their property look like this, I had no idea who lived there. It was an unusual set of circumstances that caused me to learn about who owned the place.

Out of the blue, Helen called me one day to invite Glenn and me to a dinner party at her house, making sure that I understood exactly where she lived. I assured her that I knew precisely where her house was and explained that I never went by it without spending some time admiring it. Before ending the conversation, she further explained that we had a mutual friend in the town where I once had lived and that friend had told her about me. Therefore, after talking with my friend recently, she and W.L. had decided to include us in their next dinner party group. What a nice gesture, considering that we had never officially met, but I was very excited because this meant that I would get to see the interior of that house I had admired from the street since arriving in town.

There were some flowers growing at that time on the property, which would become Chinaberry Ranch, and I thought it would be a nice gesture to cut some of those and take them with us when we went to dinner. Little did I know that this would be the epitome of a "coals to Newcastle" situation! I had no idea that W.L. was the flower person to surpass all flower people, having the best of talent as far as arranging and coordinating flowers with decor, being a bonsai expert and maintaining his yard to perfection. His reputation as an expert floral designer stretched back over many years in this town. I would soon learn about his expertise when I showed up at the dinner party with my country arrangements of cosmos, garden roses and other varieties—the interior of his house was decorated with fresh cut flowers everywhere, arranged as if the state garden club competition were being held there.

Introductions were made, conversations were begun, and the evening turned from pleasant to even more pleasant. Because the house was not a large spread-out place, but rather a small, cozy design that lent itself to feelings of comfort and warmth, the gathering quickly took on a festive and fun atmosphere, with everyone talking and laughing at the same time. No one was too busy, however, to notice the aroma coming from the kitchen, a blend of food odors that made all of us know the dinner would be wonderful. It was possible to tell from the smells flooding the house that someone had spent many hours preparing this dinner and making delicious casseroles, perfectly blended salad dressings and desserts that were of the heavenly variety.

While everyone was enjoying pre-dinner cocktails, I had time to observe the beautiful furnishings and tastefully done decor of the house. There were objects of interest and beauty everywhere I looked. Every tabletop was filled with unusual cut glass, china, brass and silver in the form of trays, vases and picture frames. To accumulate this number of lovely pieces, the couple had to have spent long hours, which turned into long years of searching and buying, finding just the kind of decorative item for just the proper place in this house. The amazing thing about all of this stuff was that it all fit so well in the small house without looking in the least bit crowded or out of place. The walls were covered with numerous pictures, sconces and mirrors, which added color and excitement to the beauty that was displayed everywhere else, making the overall effect one of overpowering loveliness. Throughout the house were examples of W.L.'s bonsai. Mingled with the other lovely things were small trays and shallow bowls with the most beautiful jade trained by the patient hand of this man. Before I had had a chance to take all of this in, we were called to dinner.

The dining table was a picture-perfect setting with one of W.L.'s flower arrangements holding court in the center of the highly polished silverware and gorgeous china. We took our seats, as instructed by the place cards, and the meal began, a meal to remember with all the delightful tastes one could imagine. There was a delicious seafood casserole, which was combined with perfectly cooked vegetables, and the best homemade biscuits, not to mention a scrumptious bread pudding with brandy sauce for dessert. The look of sheer delight on all the guests' faces made it unnecessary for us to make any comment about the flavor and taste of each dish, and, in addition, the entire group was eagerly moving the forks from plates to mouths in such a way that there could be no mistake about our degree of enjoyment.

As I glanced around the table at the group, I thought what a wonderful gift to give to friends like us: this delightful food, beautiful flowers and objects of art, housed in the perfect setting of these people's house. To be invited to one of these dinner parties was equivalent to presenting someone with an elegant gift, a gift that would be next to impossible to find anywhere else but here in this house with these people who were entertaining us. While I was in the act of making this observation, it came to me why all of this worked so well. The coordination of the food, wine, flowers, house, yard and other components of the perfect dinner party could be pulled off with this efficiency only if the two people doing it worked in complete harmony, like a well-oiled machine.

That's what the two of them love to do: invite friends in to enjoy all their efforts at making a beautiful display, one in which the eye is pleased, the taste buds are satisfied and the soul is rested after being a part of the event. It was almost like going on a short vacation. That setting made me think of Iceland poppies. Being with all of these different people sitting around a beautiful table, enjoying the fruits of a couple who work in perfect harmony, was just like seeing a field of different colored poppies enjoying a bright sunny day in spring.

After a couple of years, I would have an occasion to take a large bunch of Iceland poppies by their house, which I now jokingly referred to as "The Shrine" because of the way they kept the place, everything always perfect. It was, after all, so well maintained that Buddha or any other god would be happy to have it as a memorial to him. The reason I was taking the multicolored poppies by there was simply because I knew just how much W.L. and Helen would enjoy them. These flowers are not usually grown in this area of the country, and I knew that it would be a special treat for the couple to enjoy. Giving them the poppies would also provide me with an opportunity to tell them how much their dinner parties are like the beautiful fields of "champagne bubble" poppies blowing in the breeze under a clear spring sky. They truly loved the flowers, and every spring they ask when I will have some more of them.

A Few Facts About Poppies

Common name: Iceland poppy
Botanical name: *Papaver*
Size: 12-48 inches
Type: annual
Light: full sun
Origin: Asia, Greece
Soil: moist, fertile
Description: Although there are many kinds of poppies, including the illegal kind, the Iceland poppy is the most beautiful because of the delicate and varied colors of the flower, ranging from pale yellow, coral, light pink and dark pink to a crystalline white. The petals of the blooms are broad and crinkly, resembling crushed silk. Like on most other poppies, the blooms are supported on very slender, wavy stems, and the first stage of the bloom is a round, fuzzy ball, which opens rather quickly. In fact, I have seen tightly closed blooms in the morning, and by afternoon, these blooms will have opened completely.

ⳍⳍ

SO WHEN I see a large group of Iceland poppies, I am always reminded of W.L. and Helen's beautiful dinner parties because the full bloom of each person who is lucky enough to be invited to that table is very much like the loveliness I see in the silky multicolored poppies when the bright spring sun displays them in their best fashion. The hard work involved and the beauty W.L. and Helen create at their dinner parties make individual differences become less prominent and make everyone's peculiarities melt into the fun of conversation, tasty food and the pleasure of the moment. Just like a group of Iceland poppies, the dinner party is a display of people showing off their best colors and interacting with each other to enjoy the evening to its fullest.

When W.L. and Helen celebrate their seventy-fifth wedding anniversary and are asked the question "To what do you owe the success of your marriage?" the answer will not be the standard one. They will of course mention the usual answers—love, respect and honesty—but the real answer will come in one word: *beauty*. Their lives were intertwined in a quest for beauty in all things, including people.

Toady:
The Gomphrena Lady

Toady and her charming personality are woven so intricately through the fabric of this small town that one would have to believe an expert needle craftsman had performed the task. She, in her own words, claims to have lived a long life and "accomplished nothing." If marriage, child rearing, financial success, fame and power are the benchmarks of accomplishment, then Toady might be labeled an underachiever. However, a better means of testing would certainly include a "person-to-person" litmus test of sorts. Toady's true talent is filling in the gaps. By this I mean she possesses that rare and unusual talent which allows her to communicate with the old and young, the smart and not-so-smart, the rich and poor, old friends and strangers, and the list goes on and on.

Let's start with how Toady came to be known as "Toady." The story she related to me went something like this:

"When I was around thirteen or fourteen years old, there were two other girls in the classroom at school whose names were Ann, and every time our teacher called on one of us, we were very confused as to which one she was addressing. So we came up with a plan. We decided to take the dictionary down and let the book fall open on its own, providing a page from which to select a random nickname. Of course, we agreed that our eyes would be tightly shut at this point. Then one of us would take a pointed index finger and run down the page to a stopping point. There would be the word that might be used to replace our legitimate name and eliminate the confusion of having three girls named Ann. My finger rested on the word "Toady" and I have been generally known by that moniker ever since the beginning of my teens."

After hearing her tell this story, I went to my Webster's and found the following definition for the word "toady": "A person who flatters or defers to others for self-serving reasons; a sycophant."

More interesting than the definition that I found was the lengthy word history: "The earliest recorded sense (around 1690) of toady is 'a little or young toad,' but this has nothing to do with the modern usage of the word. The modern sense has rather to do with the practice of certain quacks or charlatans who claimed that they could draw out poisons. Toads were thought to be poisonous, so these charlatans would have an attendant eat or pretend to eat a toad and then claim to extract the poison from the attendant. Since eating a toad is an unpleasant job, these attendants came to epitomize the type of person who would do anything for a superior, and toadeater (first recorded in 1629) became the name for a flattering, fawning parasite. Toadeater and the verb derived from it, toad-eat, influenced the sense of the noun and verb toad and the noun toady, so that both nouns could mean 'sycophant' and the verb toady could mean 'to act like a toady to someone.'"

The first time I was introduced to Toady, my mind was racing to understand the name, but, more importantly, how someone her age could have retained a nickname like that for all those years. Almost everyone growing up, whether early on or around the time of college, gets stuck with some kind of nickname, but few of us have it stick for very long. The occasion of this first introduction was a rather large dinner party that a mutual friend gave shortly after I moved to this area. I was standing near the front entrance with the hostess, and she was graciously introducing me to the guests as they arrived. Toward the end of the line of arrivals was a very nice and sedate-looking lady named Martha and her friend, Toady. As the two of them moved into the room, I said to the hostess, "Excuse me, did you say that lady's name is Toady?" She brushed aside my question by saying something like she would tell me later about this lady's real name. That never happened. In fact, no one ever did explain the mystery of that name until I began to put together the information for this book.

As time went by, I did learn that Toady's legitimate name was Ann Johnson. It was the strangest thing the way I found out about this. The small town social scene is a wonderful and a curious thing because every little community has its closed groups and exclusive cliques, and newcomers are included in only a limited way. Being there for many dinner parties and listening to the lore is the only way to obtain mundane information—like why Toady is called by that name. After several years, I had an occasion to write a thank you note to this "Toady" person, and I realized that I did not know her mailing address or proper name. Because she and her friend Martha were loyal patrons of the local library, I was able to obtain the mailing information from there.

It did not take a long time for me to observe that if there were a fun function going on anywhere in the town, Toady would be there. This list included fancy dinner parties, casual get-togethers, ladies luncheons, barbecues, afternoon tea parties, church and civic gatherings, and on and on. In fact, she said that her reputation is "for being invited and bringing the rest of the town with her." A large crowd is an arena for Toady to perform her best work: meeting, greeting, and, most of all, blending. I have never seen anyone who can go into a mixed group of people and talk with everyone in such a fashion that the group becomes a union of sorts, no matter the political, religious or social beliefs of those present. In fact, she not only has the talent to join the group members together in conversation, but she also makes them feel as though they belong there and can contribute to the fun. All the while, she is the one providing the entertainment with some long, drawn-out tale that if told by anyone but Toady would be labeled "boring." But because it is she doing the telling, all the guests hang on the edges of their seats and wait anxiously for her to come to the end of the scenario. It does not matter if those present have heard the story before because it isn't the story that matters. It is the storyteller and her mannerisms. She has performed this act for so long and on so many occasions that there are those who can recall years ago when she would be called on to do "Fireside Chats." The modern television talk show hosts could learn a great deal from this lady, who has been rather like a talk show host for many years.

One of Toady's favorite tales is about her convertibles. You see, she started driving automobiles almost as soon as she got the nickname—around the age of fourteen or fifteen. In 1941, very few teens owed cars, so picture this scene: a young girl with a convertible, a premature driver's license, a small town, and her fun personality. Who would not want to be riding around in that car? So it wasn't Toady who was the sycophant in this situation, but all those other teenagers who could not drive and, typical of that era, did not own cars. It is almost a true paradox that this lady had a nickname that implied being an "apple polisher," when in actuality she was the one everyone else had to fawn over. She subsequently owed a number of convertibles after that first one, and even bought one that was owned by Ty Cobb, Jr. A picture of Toady standing in front of this car is in the archives of the local museum.

Cars and traveling were related in Toady's life in more ways than one. She and a group of buddies once drove to Mexico to visit a veterinarian friend and his wife who were residing there because he had a grant to do research on hoof-and-mouth disease. Sounds like a good reason to visit to me. On another excursion, Toady and five friends drove to New York City to see some Broadway plays and other sights. She and her friend Martha once took a three-month trip around the world and visited most of the world's exotic places. Needless to say, she was not able to go by car on this particular trip. Martha said that this excursion ruined Toady because she was never quite the same after they returned home. By way of explanation, Martha said that on the trip, Toady would wake up and eagerly jump out of bed to see just what kind of fun and excitement each new place would bring. Getting back into the routine of this small town must have taken some adjusting for her. However, the compensation came when she was able to spend many hours relating the details of the trip to her friends here.

A Few Facts About Gomphrena

Common name: globe-amaranth
Botanical name: *G. globosa* and *G. haageana* species
Type: annual
Size: approximately 15 inches tall
Growth rate: very prolific and grown almost everywhere.
Description: This is not a very glamorous cut flower, but it is quite prolific and can be grown almost anywhere. There are quite a number of species, but my personal favorite is *G. haageana*, a bright red cultivar called "strawberry fields." They grow in large clumps and can be harvested as single stems, about 15 inches long, or large branches can be cut near the ground.

Welcome to my world of flowers! Consider these pictures a gift from my garden especially chosen for you.
—Robbie Williams

Front Page: zinnias in bloom.
Center Pages: (clockwise from top left) in my rose garden; a cosmos in bloom and a cosmos bud; at the market in Sandersville; at the farm; the house with Iceland poppies and viburnum in the background; brilliant roses.
Back Page: sunflowers (top); another day at the market (bottom left); Iceland poppies (bottom right).

ᘓᘔᘓᘔ

THIS FLOWER CAN blend a large arrangement of sunflowers into a harmonious treat for the eye. The red dots of the strawberry fields gomphrena add just the right amount of contrast to the arrangement to make it interesting and beautiful. When this flower is added to a formal vase of hybrid tea roses, it performs the same trick for this bouquet. I cannot think of any flower or type of arrangement that would not be more attractive if this flower were added to fill in space and accent the personality of the main components.

ᘓᘔᘓᘔ

THIS FLOWER AND Toady are most similar in what they do with their respective positions. Toady truly blends and fills in the spaces and somehow makes the whole "arrangement" of different people more fun and entertaining.

ᘓᘔᘓᘔ

AND THEN THERE was Pat.

Flowers With A Message

The gift shop at the local hospital is more like a small utility closet than a place for retail sales or the moneymaking project of pink ladies. I discovered this place, by accident, when I went to visit a hospitalized friend and stopped to purchase a card. The shop was surprisingly well stocked, given the limited space it had been allotted. There were rows of small ceramic figures, stuffed animals, every kind of candy and snack, a nice selection of cards, and even balloons of every color with varied messages printed on them. The messages read like a headline in the newspaper: "IT'S A BOY" or 'IT'S A GIRL" or a simple "GET WELL SOON." While I was there, it came to my attention that there were no fresh flowers, a scarcity that should not have surprised me given the shop's shortage of space. Coolers, large buckets and all the hardware that go with having a floral business require lots of room, not to mention the personnel to perform the duties that go along with the business. After my initial visit to the hospital, I started to think of a way that I might furnish this shop with fresh flower arrangements for the friends and families of the hospitalized and also for the staff that worked there. Realizing that refrigeration and storage would be the major drawback, I slowly entertained the possibility of transporting the arrangements on a daily or frequent basis so that space for storage would not be a problem. Not taking into account the labor intensity of this project, I set about to find out how the little shop was managed and who would be the person to make the decision about letting me try my new idea there. With just a few phone calls, I was able to find out that the shop was a "Pink Lady" volunteer project, as are most hospital gift shops. Next I obtained the name of the lady who was in charge of the buying and the staffing and maintaining of the place. Her name was Pat.

I called the gift shop on an early spring afternoon to find that Pat was working, and when I spoke with her, she said she would be more than happy to see me to discuss my idea. When I got to the little gift shop, the lady I would come to know as Pat was busy with customers, and it was a little while before she had time to hear my proposal about fresh flowers. After we had a brief discussion, she agreed that we could try a few arrangements for a trial period, provided I brought some sort of small table on which to display the arrangements. She further explained that because of their limited space inside the shop, the table would have to be placed in the corridor just outside the shop. I agreed with that condition and told her that I would bring a few flowers in on the following Monday.

Over the weekend I came up with an idea to include a small message on each of the flower arrangements: a computerized cut-out card in the shape of hearts, stars, or various other objects printed with short inspirational sayings. A typical message might say, "Prayer changes things," or "You are my sunshine," or "Thinking about you at this difficult time." I attached the card to a small bamboo stake, which was placed among the flowers in the finished arrangement. I also used a variety of colors for the paper cards—yellow, which looked nice in an arrangement of daisies and yellow roses, or red, which complemented a basket filled with white and red miniature roses, or pink, if the flowers were dainty and feminine in nature.

The "Flowers with a Message" venture went over quite well with the gift shop, the staff at the hospital and the family and friends of patients there. I carried the small arrangements into the hospital when the Pink Ladies would call to say the previous ones had sold, thereby making room for more flowers and assuring that there were fresh ones available. Because so much depended on the number of patients in the hospital or other projects going on there, predicting sales was impossible. Some days the flowers would be sold by the time I drove back to Chinaberry Ranch, and other days, I would have one or two arrangements that did not sell at all. Then there was the day the Pink Lady called, all in a snit, to say someone had stolen two of the arrangements from the table in the hall. She was extremely upset, begging for forgiveness, and hoping that I would understand that she had been so busy that she had totally missed the dirty deed. When I started to laugh, she was puzzled. I explained that I considered it the best of compliments that someone would go to the trouble to steal some of my flowers, choosing to believe that the robber found the flowers irresistible, needed them badly without having the money to buy them, or had some other desperate reason for taking them. I told her not to feel bad about the situation, and that if it became a regular happening, we could make other arrangements. It never happened again. There was, however, the time a rather flighty lady removed a single yellow rose from an arrangement and carried it around as she browsed in the shop, explaining to the Pink Lady on duty that she thought it so nice that they had free flowers for customers.

It was not long before I realized I was working too hard, getting little money and meeting myself in the road with all the going and coming from the farm to town. It took a while for me to wake up and recognize this because I became so involved in the pleasure it was bringing to the Pink Ladies and their customers, I almost forgot about the futile financial effort I was involved in. I was almost to the point of calling a halt to the project when the following story actually took place:

Coming very slowly up the dirt road to the top of the hill where Chinaberry Ranch stood in all its simple and rather ugly glory was a van driven as if the person at the wheel was not at all sure where to go or even if going up this hill were a good idea. Glenn and I happened to be out doing our routine chores when the van appeared. We were always rather surprised when a car did happen up there because the position of our place made it impossible to see from the road, and most times, people looking for us got lost.

We stopped our hoeing and digging to see that there was a rather young woman getting out of the driver's side door and several small children emerging from all the other car doors. In the woman's arms was a very tiny infant. Our first thought was that this lady must have taken a wrong turn and was here to ask for directions. However this was not the case. She asked if this were "Chinaberry Ranch," and we told her it was. We were accustomed to the look of surprise that she had on her face because visitors came here expecting a formal setting with gorgeous surroundings, especially if they had seen some of our flowers in town. The way that we grew cut flowers, which does not require any sort of pretty bushes or ornamental shrubs, did not prepare the average visitors for what they saw on their first visit here. They came expecting to see the usual lovely garden with things like azaleas, camellias, boxwoods, and all sorts of decorative shrubs. Instead, there was still plenty of evidence of the old "pig farm" mixed in with the rose bushes, sunflowers, zinnias, and other cut flowers, making Chinaberry Ranch slightly less than orderly and beautiful in basic design. It always took a few minutes for newcomers to adjust to this scenario and regain their shock at what they saw. However, when they did refocus, they were most of the time rather pleased with the arrangement.

This particular lady seemed more pleased than most of our first-time visitors because she was more interested in having us see her baby than in her seeing anything we were growing. She almost thrust the child towards us as if to say, "Can you believe this miracle?" And then she started explaining. It seemed that a year or so before, she had been pregnant with her third child, when disaster came in the way of a miscarriage late in the second trimester. During her hospitalization, she had received some "Flowers with a Message" arrangements from her friends and family. She said she had kept the message cards from the arrangements after the flowers had died, placing them in with her other belongings, which she took home from the hospital stay. After putting away her other things from the suitcase, she placed the "messages" on her night table, not having decided what to do with them.

She told us that she and her husband went through a rather rough time, and she particularly became very depressed after losing the child. However, from time to time, she would come across the "messages," telling her that "Prayer changes things" and "God loves you." Somewhere along the line, she began to read the sayings on a daily basis and slowly began to feel better after she read them. What she seemed to be saying was that her outlook improved as a result of the "messages" and her daily devotion to them.

Several months later she became pregnant again, much to her delight. And every day she continued to do her "message' devotions, trying to overcome any fears that they might lose this baby, too. The healthy baby came, dissolving all that depression, fear and doubt. So, this lady was here with that baby, exuding pride, smiling like a sunflower and giving credit where credit was probably not due. She had gone to the trouble to look us up, had driven the twenty miles out here, and wanted us to know just how important the "Flowers with a Message" were to her and her family. She further prevailed upon me never to stop doing the hospital arrangements because, in her words, "You can never know when the messages might make a huge difference in someone's life, as it had in mine."

We had a nice visit with her and her children. They had a fun time roaming around the place, even picking a few flowers to take home. After the van had disappeared down the drive, I thought long and hard about her conversation. Maybe I would continue to do the arrangements for the hospital gift shop, at least for the time being.

Another reason for continuing to do the flowers for the Pink Ladies was the pleasant interchange I had with them. Every time I entered the front door of the hospital, the ladies on duty at the front information desk always had pleasing comments about the flowers, and the ones working in the shop seemed to get lots of pleasure from just having the flowers around to look at and smell. But Pat was the person most thrilled with the setup.

Pat was the real mover and shaker for that gift shop project. Her personality was the perfect blend of enthusiasm, efficiency and heart to make the thing work and work well. Sometimes when I would take the arrangements, she would be working in the shop, and there would be no customers around. Those were the times we had fun little chats about all sorts of things, but mainly about her project and the great interest in the scholarship fund they worked on. The Pink Ladies of the hospital auxiliary, ably led by Pat, remind me of vines of sweet peas that have a single-minded purpose of climbing high and producing the best of everything within their possibilities. A single sweet pea bloom is nice, but to enjoy the fragrance and beauty of the plant, a mass of them is necessary. The Pink Ladies, just like the large grouping of sweet peas, do their work as a group and give their best efforts to the strength of their cause.

A Few Facts About Sweet Peas

Common name: sweet pea
Botanical name: *Lathyrus odoratus*
Type: annual vine
Size: to 6 feet tall
Origin: Italy
Light: full sun
Soil: loose, moist, fertile and well-drained
Growth rate: fast
Description: Sweet pea blooms are produced on a fast-growing vine that can be rather tall, depending on the region in which they are grown. The blooms can be a wide range of colors—pink, purple, lavender, white, red and yellow—and

best of all, they have the most wonderful fragrance of any flower. They prefer cooler weather as a home, but they can be grown in the South, if they are planted in the winter and fall. Usually the winters are mild enough to keep them from freezing. Anyone who has the opportunity to walk past a fence loaded with blooming sweet peas on a warm spring day and can catch a whiff of their perfume will forever be in love with the flower. The vines have rather flat stems, which have delicate little tendrils that grab onto anything that is nearby, making it possible for the vine to become a strong clinger, almost impossible to tear it away from its purpose.

Fly, Fly Away

After a couple of years, the flowers were blooming excessively, the bamboo was shooting to the sky, and things were generally moving along fine. While I was becoming more and more involved with the flowers and terra firma, Glenn was becoming tired of the heavy work schedule on the farm added to his regular job at the hospital. Being a full-time urologist and a part-time farmer made him very busy. This change of heart was not sudden, but it did take place without my being aware of it because my enthusiasm for the ground and the flowers it produced overshadowed almost everything. That's the way life is, I guess. When one person becomes so totally involved with something, she mistakenly thinks her partner is having the same thrills and emotions as she, when in actuality, that is sometimes not true. Therefore, learning about Glenn's disillusionment with gardening came as a complete shock to me on that early spring afternoon when he told me about his next move.

We were sitting on the deck on the back of the house admiring all the products of our labors, when he announced that he was going to buy an airplane. I hate flying almost as much as I love dirt. So his announcement was horrifying for more reasons than one. First of all, I had mistakenly presumed that he considered the flower business something of value and worthwhile, rather than a burden. Secondly, I had only heard him talk about flying on a few occasions and knew for a fact that during his previous marriage of nineteen years, he had never flown an airplane. Some time back, he had briefly mentioned that when he was in college, he had taken flying lessons and had gotten his private pilot's license. I even remember his telling me about a small plane he had owned for a short time when he was in his residency, but that had been many, many years ago. How could this mature, gray-haired, supposedly intelligent person even entertain the idea of flying again after so many years and no contact with the sport? The answer to this question was forthcoming. He explained that he was tired of the farming process and needed to have a hobby that had nothing to do with farming or medicine. Of course, I took this as an insult to all that had gone on at Chinaberry Ranch.

Another part of the puzzle came into place when he further explained that he had been visiting the local airport in his spare time. One of the best assets of this small, central Georgia town where we lived was the airport because for a town this size, the airport was exceptional. The lore was that it had been built many years ago as part of a military installation and afterward, the government had turned it over to the locals in the town. Being "infected" is a term not just used in medicine, but it is how former pilots refer to their past addiction to flying. Let me tell you—I was soon to learn how very serious this addiction can be. The airplane is a complex machine and requires long hours of time and study to fly it, but somewhere in this procedure, an addiction like no other occurs. I was led to believe that once this illness overcomes someone, it lies there silently for years, even if the pilot is away from flying for a long time. Not only does it lie there, but also it can be totally revived with only the slightest exposure to an aviation setting. Glenn's explanation of his latest attack from the sleeping fly bug did little to assuage my hurt and disappointment.

There were days of breakdowns in communication between us in which I searched for an answer to my dilemma. These are the times in life when all of your past decisions are brought into question, and the doubt about your ability to make another decision is there like a massive rock, waiting to be moved out of your way. It was during such a time that I was reminded that I also had had an addiction at one time. About ten years before this, I had had a disease called golf, but I was not sure that it could be revived as easily as the flying malady. During my life before Glenn and Chinaberry Ranch, I had been an avid golfer with a low handicap. To achieve this level of expertise in that game while being a full-time wife and mother, I was required to work extremely hard and devote long hours to it. There had been a time when I would have said to anyone who asked, "Golf is my best friend, and I will never stop playing it!" My involvement with Glenn had changed all of that because he considered golf not as a friend, but almost as an enemy. He had played since his teenage years but had found that the patience the game requires was not something he could summon on the golf course. To the contrary, his personality on the course turned into that of a madman when confronted with certain golf shots. Consequently, we had not played much together in the last few years, and I had elected to devote most of my time to the flowers and the ranch. It was strange that at that moment of disappointment and hurt, the first thing I had thought about going back to was golf. I guess I was a little like Scarlet of *Gone With The Wind* with her decision to always "go back to Tara." And so Glenn went back to flying and I went back to golf.

He bought the airplane of his dreams, a bright red and white Citabria with that wonderful "tail dragger" wheel. But that was only the beginning. This plane had more hidden problems than the average used car, and the re-covering of the wings, the repair of certain engine parts, and just keeping it flying was a full-time job. But unlike a car that needs constant repairs and causes problems for the owner, a plane with problems is a blessing. That is, according to Glenn, because all these repairs allow you to spend time and lots of it with that wonderful machine. I have learned over the years to appreciate the fact that flying fanatics really don't care if the plane isn't in the air, just as long as they are with the plane. I do not think I have ever heard a pilot get upset when he had to have his plane in the hangar for repairs, especially when that pilot could be in on the repair job.

I got out the golf clubs, dusted them off, looked for my other equipment and tried to remember how to swing those old clubs. The first thing I was confronted with was realizing right away that golf isn't like riding a bicycle—you do forget just how to do it, and it takes a long, long time to get back to half of where you were when you stopped playing. One afternoon I was out in the field swinging a golf club when I remembered a little golf course nearby where I had played a few times when I lived in Augusta. It was in a town about twenty-two miles to the north of Chinaberry Ranch, a town called Sandersville. I had played the course only three or four times but remembered fondly the setting and the layout of the place. I decided to check it out within the next few days.

On one of the next weekends when Glenn was going to spend the entire time at the local airport doing some of those repairs, I decided to travel to the course in Sandersville. But sometime before that trip, I had started to think about the fact that maybe there would be some outlet for flower sales in that town. That way, I could kill two birds with one stone, if I decided to pursue the golf and spend some time there. So, bright and early on that Saturday morning, I took off on my adventure. Little did I know what an adventure it would turn out to be! Upon arriving near the town, I remembered that the golf course was located out from the town some distance and decided to try to find it by making a random turn, even though I wasn't at all sure of the correct way to go. Before too long, I began seeing a golf hole running parallel to the highway, and then I realized that my memory had been correct because when I had played there years before, this hole had stuck in my mind vividly. The reason for this memory was not pleasant; to the contrary, it was rather unpleasant because I had sliced my tee shot into the highway on which I was traveling at the moment. I turned into the parking lot, looked for a space to park and sat there looking around at totally unfamiliar surroundings. The last time I had been there, there had been just a small concrete block clubhouse, but now there was an extremely nice-looking brick building, which I could tell was not very old. After some time, I went into the pro shop to ask about the rules they had about playing there. I knew that some small towns had rather lenient rules about membership and the play on their course by those who were not members. A large number of these small clubs in this area need the extra money they derive from allowing non-members to play, making it relatively easy to get in a few rounds of golf with very few restrictions. So I went into the clubhouse to find the pro shop.

There was not much activity in the pro shop that day. In fact, the only person in there was a kind, older gentleman behind the counter who explained the fees and rules about play, assuring me all the while that they would be happy to have me play almost any time. This was good news to me because it would give me the opportunity to see if I were going to get back into golf on a full-time basis or if I wanted to just investigate the possibilities. Either way, I felt welcome to go in any direction I chose. And then too, having played there some years ago, I did not feel like a complete stranger, even though I knew no one there at this time. The nice gentleman further explained that there was a small practice area, which was hidden behind a large hedge of photinia bushes, located a short distance from the shop. This situation was a definite improvement over most practice areas I had been to because the people sitting in the club house could not see the person hitting balls on the practice area, making practice a totally private event. I had been to many clubs where watching golfers as they practiced was a form of entertainment for the staff and people in the clubhouse, making some shy beginners most uncomfortable. I decided to take the man up on his offer to use the practice tee to hit a few balls and soon was on my way down the curved path to the photinia-hidden practice tee. Although I did not hit the balls very well, I did enjoy being "back in the swing" of things again. I suddenly realized that I truly had been missing my old friend—"Golf."

There were a few more of these trips to this place, a few rounds of golf, and several practice tee sessions in the next months. Finally one day, after I had finished walking nine holes, this same kind guy said to me, "You know, you really should join this club. It would be a lot cheaper for you, and we have a special membership drive on now. It would only cost you a three hundred dollar initiation fee, with seventy dollar per month dues." I told him that I would think about it, and the next time I was over there, I would talk to the manager about it. On the way home, I could not get those low figures out of my mind, and the rest of the day, I was mulling over the idea of joining that little club. The golf bug had taken over by that time, and it was an easy decision to make. An application form was the next step, and I knew that I would probably be filling one out pretty soon. My rationale had something to do with the idea of disciplining myself about using the place to make myself invest the time and energy to play golf well again. Knowing that I had joined the club would make me use the club and consequently would force me to make room in my schedule for the time that golf takes in order to play moderately well.

I spoke with the manager on my next trip to the course and filled out the necessary paperwork in order to apply for membership. This application form was not very complicated and did not require much in the way of recommendations or involved information. After giving the manager a check for the initiation fee, I asked him how long before I could play as a member and when the application would be approved so that I could use the other membership privileges. He reminded me that they ran a very small operation there and that it would be only a few days before I would have full membership status. Sure enough, within a few days, I was a full-fledged member of the club. I did not share this exciting news with Glenn because he was extremely busy with his airplane and probably would not have heard me had I told him. Besides, it was more than just a little bit of fun to have my secret all to myself for a while, knowing that it would be more of a "gotcha" the longer I was able to keep the news from him.

The way the news was broken to him was rather interesting. We had a couple over for dinner a few weeks later, and as the conversation turned to golf, because they were golfers, I casually mentioned that I had begun playing golf again. They insisted that I come play as their guest at their club, all the while very excited that I had returned to my old hobby. I told them I would love to play as their guest, but they, too, would have to come to my new club to play as my guests someday soon. After a rather long silence, Glenn spoke up and asked me to repeat my last sentence, or asked something like, "What did you say?" It was then that I explained my new membership in the Sandersville club, relating all the history as well as the recent events. My justification for the renewed interest in my old hobby was explained by the story of Glenn's recent purchase of an airplane that required long hours to repair and maintain. The couple was already aware of his buying a plane, but no one at the dinner table was aware that I had taken up golf again until I told them that night.

If the truth be known, I think Glenn was exceedingly glad that I had begun to play golf and had joined a club because men sometimes feel a little guilty about their toys and the time they take playing with them. Having women in their lives who are preoccupied with their own hobbies or activities makes their lives just a little easier. A relationship between two people is always strengthened if each of them has a few things that are done individually rather than together. I simply cannot imagine what some couples find to talk about if they are together most of the time; their interests would be so intertwined that scintillating conversation must be next to impossible.

Little did I know that this return to golf would be just the beginning of my adventures in Sandersville. There was a whole new world waiting for me in that rustic little town.

Part 2

Sandersville

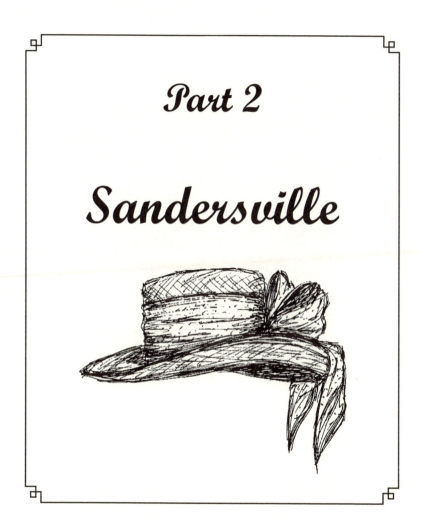

The Square

The first time I saw the courthouse square in Sandersville, I fell in love with it, partly because it was the picture-perfect, small Southern town classic square, resembling in some ways all of the other courthouse squares in all of the other small Southern towns, but in a mysterious way, markedly different. Something about the positioning of the building and the architectural design of it caught the eye and dared the onlooker to turn away, or caused the person to turn back for a second glance had he turned away. I decided the boldness of the building was further emphasized by the fact that it seemed almost too big for the square that surrounded it; even though it seemed too big, at the same time, it seemed appropriate. This paradoxical setting coupled with the businesses that completely circled the square made one think of a very close-knit family gathering, or reunion, one that was ongoing and never-ending. Even though some of the business fronts were not coordinated—some modern in facade, some older-looking, made of everything from concrete blocks to brick, painted various colors ranging from bold to bland, and extending in sizes that went from tiny to grand—the differences in the store fronts did not seem to distract from the uniformity of the square, but on the contrary, gave the place a special charm, as if having no strict plan in the beginning was a blessing rather than a bother.

A blessing rather than a bother was exactly the feeling a person got when visiting the square, extremely inviting and totally welcoming. This setting and these combined buildings arranged in this fashion were all the welcoming committee that was necessary to make one feel comfortable. Maybe this feeling was fostered by all of the busy activities that had gone on there for so many years before, all the legal dealings in the large courthouse, the trading and swapping in the area around the building, and the setting up of businesses near the area. Ghosts from past generations and the dealings of these old settlers could be felt by just approaching the area of the downtown section. This feeling is not apparent in all small towns, but the ones that do have this marvelous asset generally have done little to promote it. It is a natural occurrence that cannot be programmed. It is as though those people from the past still linger in small nooks and crannies, watching the area as if it were still their duty to protect it from harm.

This particular courthouse and the square surrounding it have a history of disaster. The original courthouse was built in 1796 when Sandersville was made the county seat. However, the building was destroyed by a fire, which almost burned the entire town down along with the courthouse. Another courthouse was erected in 1856, but unfortunately, it was in the path of General Sherman's "March to the Sea," and he ordered that it be burned to the ground, destroying everything but the walls. The present-day courthouse, built in 1869, has undergone changes and renovations at different times over the past years. Maybe the long history of disaster associated with this area of town has caused a deep appreciation of it and made the citizens of the town take special pride in their square.

It was quite by accident that I came to this courthouse square one cold winter day. After playing golf, I had a conversation with some ladies about my flower business, and I asked them if they knew of any way that I might market some of my fresh-grown cut flowers in the community. A couple of the women said that there was a farmer's market of sorts at the courthouse square downtown on Saturday mornings, and they suggested that I investigate this possibility. They were not sure about the rules and regulations or the times when this kind of market took place, but they suggested that I might just ask one of the merchants with a business on the perimeter of the square. They did know that the market was limited to Saturday mornings only.

The following Saturday I drove to the downtown area

to see if there were any sign of vendors in the square, but I saw only a few cars and very little else going on. On a street corner opposite the square, I spotted an antique shop that appeared to be open for business. So I entered the shop and asked the nice lady behind the counter about the Saturday farmer's market situation, making sure that she understood that I knew very little about it. In fact, I explained that I did not even know for certain that there was such a thing as a farmer's market there. She said she knew that they had something like that, but she suggested that I ask the lady standing behind the blue station wagon over in the parking lot of the courthouse square. The antique shop owner said that the woman she was pointing out was a regular on Saturdays because she baked cakes and sold them every week, having a regular clientele as well as new customers all the time. I thanked the shopkeeper, said good-bye and walked toward the person selling cakes from her car. This is how I came to know Sadie.

Sadie

It was not yet spring, still slightly chilly, but a brilliant sunny day when I first met Sadie. When I approached her spot in the parking area of the square, she was engaged in conversation with a nice-looking couple. They could have been there only to buy a cake, but I got the impression they were also her friends. I hesitated a bit to give them a chance to finish their talk, but they saw that I wanted to approach them, so they stopped talking and greeted me in a most friendly fashion.

The blue station wagon, with the back tailgate down, was facing the street, and directly behind it was a card table with a red-and-white checked tablecloth on it. On this table was an array of the most beautiful, delectable cakes I had ever seen. Caramel, chocolate, coconut, hummingbird, key lime and red velvet were some of the kinds I could see shining under their covers. Looking beyond the table, into the back of the car, I could see what looked like an ocean of cakes, lining the entire back of the station wagon. I was completely overcome with this display of talent and hard work. It prompted me to ask her if she had made all of these cakes by herself, or if she had had any help. She assured me that she made all of them from "scratch," explaining that some were special orders and others were just for the random buyer. The couple standing nearby explained that her reputation was such that she had a regular trade, and those loyal customers were always bringing new customers.

Introductions were made between us, and she told me that her name was Sadie, but she was also known as the "Cake Lady." That was certainly understandable. To make her job seem even more commendable, she explained that she did not live in Sandersville, but in a small community about fifteen miles away and made the extra effort of transporting all those delicate, edible items. I was tired just hearing about this kind of human endeavor, but the amazing thing was that she didn't seem tired or the least bit burdened by this mobile cake business. She almost appeared refreshed and happy, rather than tired and sad, and most of all, she seemed to be enjoying the whole process. Having grown up in a household in which my mother made these kinds of cakes on special occasions and for special people, I could completely relate to the kind of work and effort that went into the baking of a homemade cake, or, as we say in the South, a cake made from "scratch." Somewhere in this conversation, she made a nonchalant comment about her age, not in a complaining style, but rather proud and pleased to do this amount of work at age seventy-five. The word that came to my mind was "unbelievable." I could not imagine being able to accomplish this task at my age, given that I was ten or fifteen years her junior. Forget trying to do this kind of thing at her age.

The combination of the gray hair and very pleasant expression on her face made me think of the picture-perfect way grandmothers would look if we all could create our own grandmothers. But this was not the real secret to her overall pleasing appearance. It was her manner that made you want to talk with her, do business with her and, most of all, just stand near and watch. In other words, she was the kind of person passersby loved to talk with, even if they did not buy a cake. Along with the pleasant expression on her face, she had a rather soft voice that spoke of all things in the same way, making bad news seem okay and good news sound even better than it was.

After a while, I told her that I raised fresh cut flowers on a farm nearby and needed a place to sell them when there was an overflow of blooms, and that someone had told me that there was a farmer's market in this square on Saturday mornings. She explained that the information was correct, but the activity was usually limited to the warm months of the growing season. However, in her case, she was there almost every Saturday morning. Because the weather had not yet warmed up and growers had not started to come, her cake business was about the only business being conducted while I was talking with them. She said that the market was started to try to encourage people to come to the downtown area on Saturdays and to provide the people in town with some fresh produce, baked goods, other homemade and homegrown products like jams and jellies, and all kinds of crafts. When I inquired about any rules and regulations that might govern the place, she said that the homegrown stipulation was the only one. Getting there very early was a requirement if you wanted to have one of the chosen spots, that is, a spot under the shade of a tree or in the most heavily trafficked area. There was no fee charged for vendors, and everyone provided his or her own table for display or used the back of a car or truck to sell from.

We spent a little more time chatting and passing the time of day about things in general, but soon I told them that I should be getting back home, thanked them for all their help and left them in the square to resume their previous conversation. As I drove away, I looked in the rear view mirror at the three of them and wondered what they thought of some stranger coming around and asking questions about the square, particularly asking about selling cut flowers, but they appeared in my mirror to have taken up their conversation, and the situation seemed unaltered, as if I had never interrupted them.

On the twenty-mile drive back home, I went over and over in my mind the talk we had had and thought about all those cakes and all that hard work. But most of all, I thought about the kind eyes, soft voice and gentle manner of the "Cake Lady," making me think that I would enjoy the Saturday morning activities of the square. By the time I reached my house, I was pretty sure that I would be taking my flowers in the spring to sell in the courthouse square. In fact, it was something that I was looking forward to with a great deal of eager anticipation. I thought I would enjoy the company of Sadie and other vendors, the appreciative customers and the adventures that go with being in the open-air market. Before going inside the house, I detoured by some flower beds to check for the upcoming blooms, but I found that the plants were still sleeping and knew that it would be some time before I would be able to try my hand at selling flowers in the square of Sandersville.

Spring And Eternal Hope

Seed catalogs are one of life's nicest gifts. This is not just because of the pretty pictures and colorful displays or the format in which the catalogs are done, but also rather because of the timing of their arrival. Winters in the South can be bleak and colorless, even though there is little bitter cold, that kind of cold that characterizes the North and other parts of this country. There are many days when the sun doesn't shine, and the wind blows with such ferocity that we Southerners think we have been mysteriously transported to another part of the United States, sort of like Dorothy in *The Wizard of Oz*. Some long periods of cold are broken with a few days of spring-like weather, but then a front brings another round of extremely cold wind and no sunshine. Because we are spoiled here below the Mason-Dixon line, these periods of dreary weather do not sit well with us, particularly when they last a long time and do not have those pleasant warm interruptions. But sometime after Christmas and before Easter, all of us gardeners start to go to the mailbox with a renewed sense of purpose: we are looking for those wonderful seed catalogs.

It is truly a blessing that the seed companies send their catalogs out at different times because getting a tax bill, a utility bill and Christmas bills interspersed with a seed catalog is like taking medicine with a spoonful of sugar. When I reach into the dark domain of the mailbox and feel the glossy cover of a magazine-type object in there, the anticipation starts to build because I am certain that this could be one of those magical tomes that lets me know spring is just around the corner. Living about five hundred yards from the mailbox, which is situated on the highway, makes going to get the mail somewhat of a treat any time of the year, but especially around January and February. I am constantly reminded of this thrill when I make a trip into a local town and observe along the way little old ladies making their way to their mailboxes. As I pass by, I always say a little prayer that they will find one of those beautiful seed catalogs in with their other mail. I watch these ladies as they move with a little bit of speed to get their mail, but then on the route back to their houses, they move slowly so that they can go through the mail, being unable to wait until they are inside to see if there is something good, like a seed catalog. Being a gardener makes going to the mailbox a worthwhile experience because hope is always a good thing.

After the miscellaneous mail has been put away and a comfortable chair found, it is time to kick back and dream. A seed catalog for the real grower is not like reading a magazine or any other print material, but rather it is a very slow and deliberate process, a process whereby every inch of every page is committed to the eye for enjoyment, and every picture causes the reader to stop to dream for a little while. The buying process is entirely different from the spring picture shopping done when the catalog first arrives. Turning those pages at the start is a soul-reviving endeavor, having nothing to do with what may or may not be bought later on. It is almost like a CPR maneuver for the wintertime blues. In fact, I have heard about people who never order from these catalogs but will talk at length about spending hours looking at the contents in the late winter just so they will feel better. Hope starts with the seed catalog and builds from there, making readers think that they will somehow this year do things differently, or grow something they haven't grown before, or maybe just dream about a certain flower on page ten. Every year when the winter wind howls and the sun is hidden away, I think of those people who might not be getting these beautiful seed catalogs, and I put them on my prayer list.

After meeting Sadie in the square, I was especially eager about every little catalog that came in the mail, and it was with more anticipation than usual that I carefully looked through them. Realizing that someone who might not know the name of a certain flower or might have never grown anything could possibly be one of my customers at the square made the joy of seed shopping a special thing that first year before my initial trip to the square.

Deciding what to eliminate from the order was the big problem. Page after page of brightly colored zinnias, sunflowers of every size and shape, gorgeous gladiolus, and roses of all kinds were just a few of the plants that I longed to grow for my prospective buyers. Of course, I really wanted to grow one of every flower on every page, but the elimination process was somewhat guided by what would grow in my part of the country, or I would have never been able to make a decision about the order. I was fortunate at the time to be aware of certain characteristics of flowers that made them desirable as cut flowers, like vase life and color stability. Learning what would be appropriate to grow in my region and how it would perform as a cut flower took many hours of tedious reading. So when choosing flowers from the catalog, I had to take into account things other than just the beauty or the kind of plant. I had to make sure I curbed my runaway desire to grow all things for all people, and I had to be sensible about my choices as far as the growing zone and the tricky characteristics of the plants. Just like people, plants have personalities that have to be considered if there is to be a good relationship between the grower and her little seedlings. Child rearing is a great trainer for the growing of plants. Everyone who has had more than one child knows full well the vast differences in children, even though the children are from the same parents and have been nurtured in the same environment. This pattern of differences reflects exactly how the growing process is.

After making my careful selections, I waited impatiently for the orders to arrive. There was a certain kind of disappointment in getting seeds as opposed to the ordering of them because after looking at the lovely pictures in the books, there was a little bit of shock when the order came through the mail in small envelopes and sacks. Those images from the printed catalog still remain in your head, so the arrival of the tiny seeds jars the mind, making the realization of all the hard work to come a frightening prospect. The thought of making those tiny seeds become like the pictures in the catalogs all of a sudden took on new meaning for me, a meaning filled with a certain amount of fear and trepidation. It seemed like a long way from the minuscule, hard seed to the production of a mature plant with a gorgeous bloom. I held a few of these unattractive, dried objects in the palm of my hand and meditated for a long time because it became very clear at that moment just how long that trip would be.

The hard work that would make the trip even longer had not fully registered with me, but it would not be long before it did.

Every seed envelope comes with the same warning about frost: wait until there is no longer a threat of frost before planting. The operative word here is "wait"—for that interminable period of time when the gardener is eager to get on with the process and the weather doesn't cooperate at all. Every experienced grower has tales of horror about rushing the planting program and how a late frost murdered the new seedlings, damaging the hopes for an early bloom, not to mention damaging the spirit of the hopeful gardener. We Southerners are more susceptible to this chronic impatience about early planting than folks from other parts of the country because our spring weather is so schizophrenic. We can have periods of weather in February when the temperature and weather conditions make the prospective grower think that all possibilities of frost are gone and it is safe to plant. Then the very next day, we might have temperatures down below the freezing mark. Planters, beware! The old wives' tale, if it is that, about waiting until after Good Friday to plant is the best advice, and, even then, there might be that one cold night waiting to make its appearance. But after all those dreary days of winter, the arrival of the tempting seed catalogs and the chatter with other growers about new and exciting plants, who could resist some move to get on with spring planting? All of this added to a few days of spring-like conditions, and the Southern gardener loses all patience and good judgment. I once heard about an old farmer who said that the best advice he could give about planting was to wait at least two weeks after you thought it was safe to plant and then go to it. The people who live in the frozen North and other parts of the country where the snow and ice never melt until spring has securely arrived have an easier time of it because their weather has trained them well and given them no choices.

Having gotten past the seed selection process and having unpacked the order that had arrived by mail, I was now faced with what to do with all these dried and ugly little things that I held in the palm of my hand. The instructions on the envelopes were general in nature, having to cover growing conditions of the different areas of the country in a few short sentences. So it was back to the few books I owned on gardening, and making a few more trips to the library to research the growing of certain kinds of plants. It was pretty clear that putting the seed in the ground nonchalantly was not the way to go. One of those little tricks life plays on you is lulling you into thinking that something is so very simple, when in actuality, there are millions of little facts that have to be considered and studied to avoid disaster.

Some seeds, like zinnias, could be placed directly in the soil, and that was pretty much all that was necessary. However, some had to be put in little soil containers inside the house and then transplanted later to a bigger container and ultimately, they made it to the dirt outside. Again, I was reminded that every plant, like every person, requires special treatment and has special needs. If these are ignored, disaster sets in rather quickly.

Because I now had the dream of selling cut flowers in the square in Sandersville, it was necessary to grow long rows of flowers in a small field, in addition to the beds we already had around the "pig pads." So as the warm weather came, I was busy digging in the dirt everywhere, trying to find a place to put those little, dried seeds, hoping for a big bloom later on. Turning and churning the dirt, or, as the farmers call it, harrowing, is a fun thing to see. There is something almost magical about the dark, sleepy earth being awakened in this process to produce beautiful plants and vegetables from within its warm and moist depths. Living near the soil and smelling the aroma of newly plowed dirt is an experience to savor and to keep cataloged in the mind forever because only the sights, smells and sounds of the earth being turned over and under can make us understand the mystery of how growth takes place. Maybe it's the dark brown color or the concealed warmth that lies underneath the top layer or the granular particles that envelope the tiny seed or a combination of all things working together to form a nesting place for seeds and roots that draws us to a need to communicate with the dirt. Freshly tilled soil has its own aroma like no other, and our fascination with it links us to the past and future like nothing else.

After adding a few more rose bushes to the existing ones and planting several long rows of gladiolus and many rows of zinnias and sunflowers, I waited anxiously for the big spring bloom to happen. One of the best parts of planting anything is that period between putting the seed or plant into the ground and the stage when it reaches maturity. A daily or almost-daily check is necessary just to make sure you do not miss the first growth, or to make sure you are there for the first true leaves. But mainly, it is the fun of watching every little change in the plants that counts. There is something about that constant caring for the plants that makes the whole process worthwhile because as you are waiting, caring for and watching every new stage of growth, there is a bond that takes place between you and the plants. It's this kind of link that gardeners speak about when they refer to garden therapy.

The nurturing that takes place in the garden is very much akin to the nurturing that takes place in child rearing—filled with all òf the same amounts of joy and sadness, fulfillment and disappointments, rewards and losses.

Spring finally brought forth many warm days followed by nights that began to warm up as the days got longer, giving the new flowers the conditions needed to bring the blooming process to life. And bloom they did. What a glorious sight at Chinaberry Ranch—all of the different colors and fragrances. Because of this profusion of bloom, cutting the flowers to sell seemed like just so much fun, rather than work. There were so many flowers to cut that I could stand in one spot and cut a bucketful of blooms without moving. That first bloom thrilled me so much, I never even gave a thought to the work and effort that it took to gather the flowers and make them into arrangements. I was thinking all the while of the customers in the square who would be ecstatic to have these flowers in their homes the next Saturday when I went "to market."

The First Saturday At The Square

We had bought a used van, white and inexpensive, to transport the flowers to the square on Saturdays. Removing all the seats with the exception of the fronts ones made the vehicle more than adequate to carry the arrangements and buckets of blossoms to market. After placing that amount of flowers bucket-to-bucket and positioning the arrangements close together, we stood back to admire the sight. The effect of this display was overwhelming. It is one thing to see a huge array of flowers out in an open space, but when they are crowded in a small space like the back of a van, it is breathtaking. It was such a pleasant experience to drive that van with the sights and fragrances of the cargo. The expectation of opening the back tailgate of the car, revealing all these lovely flowers to a group of appreciative people, also made the trip enjoyable.

After slowly driving to Sandersville so that the flowers did not turn over or spill out their water, we finally arrived at the square for the Saturday market, our first time on this adventure. Because it was very early, there were few people around with the exception of Sadie and a few other vendors. However, these few came running over as soon as I opened the tailgate, excitedly oohing and aahing about the display in the back of the van. The people there helped get the tables set up and the flowers arranged on them, all the while seeming truly glad that we were a part of their farmer's market venture. There was a feeling of unexplained anticipation about being out in the early morning light with other people who were hoping to have a good day mixing with their customers, just chatting about the local news, and making a little money to boot.

It was so early that the sun had hardly come from behind the buildings to the east of the square. A few more cars and a few pickup trucks came slowly into the square to find a location to set up their makeshift sales counters and to find as much shade as possible to protect their vegetables from the strong sunlight. As the people emerged from these vehicles, they all came by to admire the array of flowers we had on our tables and to ask the same questions: "Did you grow all these pretty flowers?" "Just where is your farm?" and then the best question of all—"Are these flowers real or artificial?" It came as a great surprise to me that some of these people did not understand what you meant when you said the words "cut flowers," and they always seemed to be more at ease with some sort of plant rather than a flower that would only last a few days and then die. Then after my explanation, they always asked, "Well, can I root this and make it into a plant?" It was at this point that I knew it would be necessary to educate my market in order to have sufficient people to buy my product. This was not the case, however, with all of the people there because some of the Sandersville folks were familiar with cut flowers, having lived in larger metropolitan areas where street vendors were quite common. Buying a bunch of fresh flowers on the street or at the grocery store was an everyday occurrence for these particular people. But for the few who found this a new experience, I was prepared to patiently explain the benefits of having just a few blooms in the kitchen or on the bedside table. The interesting thing about flowers, I found, was that they formed bridges in conversation, allowing differences in background and education to be overlooked and a new understanding to come from just the discussion about them. I discovered that children are always intrigued by flowers, whether boy or girl, and age is not a factor. Both young and old alike love a beautiful flower.

Everyone has heard the sayings about the eye being the door to the soul, or that it is possible to tell a lot about a person when he looks you in the eye. The eye of a person when he is taking in the beauty of a flower is a joy to watch. I have stood many times and merely watched the look in a person's eyes as he is gazing at some of my flowers and wondered he were aware of how much his facial expression changed in the process of just looking at a certain flower. Before I started selling flowers, I had thought women were the ones who loved flowers and that men sort of thought of them as a feminine thing, but after only a few trips to the square, I found that the opposite was true. It was the men who really appreciated the beauty of them. It wasn't just that they were buying them to please wives or girlfriends. Indeed, I had some regular customers who came every Saturday to buy flowers—usually more men than women—just because they really liked flowers.

That first Saturday at the square was a success, not because of the money we made, but because the people who came were so appreciative. Even those who did not buy flowers had a good time just looking, and that was perfectly all right with us. All the time you are growing, raising and harvesting flowers, the main thought in your mind is that people will look at them and enjoy them whether they buy them or not. Not only will they look at them, but also they will remember them for a long time. Some of my warmest memories are about people who came back months later and asked about a certain flower I had, wanting to know all about it and saying how much they had thought about it after being at the square. Isn't it a wonderful thing to know that some of life's unpleasantness was crowded out of someone's mind by a memory of a flower? Had I done nothing else for that person, I felt very good about that one thing.

The courthouse tower houses an antique clock, which still works perfectly, and so it is possible to see the time from every direction because the clock has four faces. As we watched the hands on this clock approach the noon hour, we realized it was time to load up the few remaining flowers and head back to the farm. But it was with a sense of worthwhileness and purpose that we loaded up and said goodbye to the other vendors. We knew without verbally saying so that we would be back for many Saturdays to come, if not for the customers, for our own sake. We had found that the fun of direct selling a homegrown product to other people was a multifaceted experience or exchange, which did not involve money, but rather feelings and emotions.

MaMa Cat

In order to house his airplane, Glenn had to build a nice, large hangar, which to me was inappropriately placed directly behind my rose garden, but in his opinion, it was quite well placed, and nothing was wrong with the back of the hangar offering a background for my rose bushes.

The hangar was not a place I frequented or even went near most of the time, especially if I were in the middle of getting flowers ready to take to the square, but one day Glenn said he needed to show me something down there. I assured him that I had no interest in anything in the hangar, but he persisted with his nagging, and after some time, I relented and we took off. The runway and hangar were about a city block from the house, and as we ambled down toward the area, I could not possibly imagine what he wanted to show me.

An airplane has to have a large area to accommodate its huge wings, creating space under and around them, and thus near the walls of the hangar we stored various objects, like lawn mowers, extra building materials and even a small fishing boat. When we entered the building, Glenn angled off toward this boat and told me to look under the back seat of the boat. At first, I did not see anything, but then I saw a tiny animal of some sort, hidden way back in a dark corner. After moving closer, I was able to see the smallest kitten I had ever seen, a kitten that could have not been more than a few days old. Glenn explained that as he had been working on his plane a short time earlier, he saw out of the corner of his eye a large tabby cat jump from the edge of the boat and leave the hangar. That was when he went over, looked inside the boat and saw the tiny baby kitten. Obviously, the MaMa Cat had hidden her kitten in this secret place to protect it from the dangers of the wild area in which we lived. We speculated that something bad must have happened to the other kittens in the litter since there was only one remaining in the boat. While we were there, MaMa Cat did not come back and must have been out on a hunting spree, looking for food for herself in the surrounding fields.

As we made our way back to the house, I told Glenn that I did not want to be responsible for the cats, telling him that I preferred to be free from the hassle of having an animal to look after. But the main reason I did not want to be involved with the animals was a secret from my childhood that had left me with bad memories of having pets. When I was around ten years old, my older brother came home one afternoon with a stray dog following along behind him. He said he did not know where the dog came from or if the dog had an home, but she had started following him as he was walking home from his job. Never having had a pet of any kind, I took to the dog right away and thought she was a special gift for me. I named her Frisky, even though she was a mature dog and probably had a name already, but she was a new experience for me. It was only a couple of weeks before she became very fat, and we knew she must be pregnant. The bad news came when she started to have the puppies and couldn't give birth to them because of a broken hip, an old injury of some kind. All I could do was watch her die in my backyard. It left me with sad memories, and I never wanted another animal to care for.

I avoided even looking in the direction of the hangar when I was outside because I didn't want to have any connection with what might be going on with the new kitten and her mama. Every now and then, when I was out planting new spring shrubbery or doing spring maintenance, I would turn toward the hangar and sneak a peek, wondering what the situation was with the two cats, but I was scared to look for very long, knowing my nurturing and caring traits would kick in and I would be down the road to over-protecting a couple of cats. Sometimes when I looked in that direction, I would catch a glimpse of MaMa Cat stalking some kind of prey such as a field mouse. But because she was so far away,

I did not have to worry that she could know I was around. Even so, she probably was catching a glimpse of me doing whatever I was doing at that time. I say this because of what happened next.

After a week or so, I came out the back door to find MaMa Cat and her kitten in the middle of the driveway—just sitting there in a huddle—with the baby being held in the mouth of the mother cat. It was as if the two cats were issuing a news bulletin stating that they were moving from the hangar to the house area. Of course, I looked away and hoped they had not realized I had seen them. I went about my gardening chores, leaving them in the driveway and wondering what would be their next move. After a short time, I returned to go back inside and did not see the cats anywhere, but I knew they were around somewhere, close by. Later that day, I found the hiding place the mother cat had selected—under a small utility building near the back deck. I caught her sneaking under the side of the building, carrying a tiny mouse in her mouth. Although it was completely dark under there, I was able to see the baby and her mother once I knelt down on the ground near the building. The animals were now too close for me to ignore them, and it was just a matter of time before I knew I would have to give them some food. Sure enough, in a few days, I could stand it no longer—I brought out a saucer of milk for MaMa Cat. In a few more days, Baby Cat moved out from underneath the utility building, and the two cats became permanent residents of Chinaberry Ranch.

Because Baby Cat had no sibling kittens, he was forever trying to get MaMa Cat to play with him. We had found that the young kitten was male, and we had decided to call them by the names we had used before they became part of the farm family—Mama Cat and Baby Cat. They became hard-working barn cats, patrolling the area constantly, catching mice frequently. Their favorite pastime involved catching a small mouse in the barn, carrying it outside on the grass and then taking turns tossing it into the air and re-catching it over and over again. This mouse game became so interesting for me to watch that I started to think the cats performed the act just for my entertainment.

The cats' morning ritual never changed once they joined the Chinaberry Ranch staff. Almost every morning the two of them would be waiting in the kitchen window when I went into that part of the house to make the coffee. On the mornings when they were not already perched on the window ledge, they would come racing from the barn, up the twelve steps and across the deck as soon as the kitchen light came on. When I looked out at the two of them sitting there, they began singing an incessant litany of meows, loud begging meows. You see, they had trained me well. Immediately, I opened the kitchen door and poured their food into empty bowls on the deck. Some mornings they ate hardly anything but spent time twirling around my feet and legs, purring contentedly. After a while, I realized that the cats really wanted to say, "Good morning," and the dispensing of the cat food was only an excuse to get me out there. This close animal friendship was what I had been trying to avoid all along. The fear of getting too close to any kind of pet still hung in the back of my mind like a ghost ready to jump out and frighten me.

After several months had passed, the unthinkable happened. In the middle of the night I was awakened by a loud crying noise, the noise animals make when they are being threatened. Chinaberry Ranch has all kinds of coyotes, owls and other creatures that could be making the distress call, but somehow I knew that one of the cats could also be the source of the loud noise. The next morning when I went into the kitchen to make coffee, I had a sense of foreboding about looking out the window, knowing that one or both of the cats could be missing. Sure enough, MaMa Cat was the only one sitting there. She was not doing her usual meows, but she sat just looking into the kitchen as if searching for someone to help her. I went out on the deck, called Baby

Cat several times and looked in all of his usual hiding places while MaMa Cat followed closely on my heels. But he was nowhere to be found. Then I had to start to worry about the loud noise I had heard during the night, and the reality set in. MaMa Cat's baby cat had been taken by some larger animal.

She, like most mothers who lose a child, never got over it. From that day on, her personality changed, and she never was the playful cat she had been before Baby Cat was taken. Many days I would find her just staring out across the fields, looking longingly for some sign of hope. But it never came. And then one day Mama Cat was gone. I like to think that she went looking for Baby Cat and found him, and they lived happily ever after, if not here on this Earth, maybe somewhere else.

The Motorcycle Customer:
The Gladiolus Man

The area surrounding the courthouse in Sandersville was used as a parking lot during the week when government business was taking place, so there were several ways to enter and exit, making it possible to circle around the building. Therefore it was easy for cars and small trucks to come inside the square and park or just cruise through to see what was available from the vendors on Saturday mornings. It was not unusual for some people to drive right up to a vendor's spot, purchase whatever they wanted and drive away without getting out of their vehicles. However, there were times when the size of the crowd made it a little difficult to maneuver through the area, but traffic, whether the walking kind or the vehicular kind, was never much of a problem.

On a particular Saturday morning, things were getting off to a rather slow start, and the sparse number of people and cars made us wonder if the morning would bring much in the way of customers. Around ten o'clock things changed. The crowd grew larger, and people started to come to buy flowers with great eagerness. A little after ten thirty, I was aware that a beautiful Harley-Davidson motorcycle was coming into the square through the south entrance, temporarily distracting me from selling flowers. I realized that of all the people who might be there to buy flowers, the gentleman riding regally on this magnificent machine probably was not one of them. I was proven wrong.

The man on the motorcycle came to an abrupt stop right in front of the place where we had set up our stand for flowers. After getting off the bike, he came over and started to look at all the flowers with a serious, discerning eye. He was a man with a mission. Of course, there was a small crowd surrounding the Harley-Davidson, oohing and aahing, touching, and wishing it were theirs. Meanwhile it was clear to me that the man was looking for something very special in the way of flowers, unusual in a way because most men ask for advice when buying flowers. He just continued to carefully eye everything and asked no questions—nothing about price, color or name. After a while, I decided that he must know exactly what he wanted. It was about this time that he stopped in front of a big container of gladiolus—brilliant reds, yellows, purples and some variegated ones. His facial expression completely changed, and it was possible to see the pleasure coming from the slight smile on his lips. He had found what he was looking for, and the satisfaction was evident. Until now he had had very little to say, but when he came upon the beautiful glads, he remarked, "These were my dad's favorite flowers." Because he used the term "were," we knew his father must no longer be living.

The crowd milling around the motorcycle continued to examine the bike the whole time the man was busy looking for his special flowers, and the other flower customers continued to shop for their favorites. Meanwhile, I stood there wondering how this man could possibly transport these fragile blooms on that motorcycle. It was very apparent that he had a plan in mind, a plan to buy some of the glads and to take them with him on his machine. After standing there for some time looking longingly at the flowers, he said that he wanted me to select all of the bright red glads, put them into a cellophane wrap, and tie them with a ribbon. I explained that I would be happy to do that and started to separate the red glads from the other colors, putting them aside to wrap later. As I was performing this task, I kept thinking about how the blooms were going to be completely destroyed once the man mounted the motorcycle and took off with the wind blowing through the flowers. He must have known from my worried expression that I was concerned about how he was going to keep the flowers intact once he took off on the motorcycle. It was almost a hurt expression on my face after all the care I had taken to protect the flowers—from cutting to transporting and then shielding them at the square once they were on display. Of all the elements, wind is possibly the most damaging to the fragility of flowers.

As I was busy preparing the bouquet, the man moved to the crowd surrounding his bike and became involved in conversation with the people who had all sorts of questions about the machine. Now that he had his business taken care of, he seemed relieved and was eager to talk with the other customers gathered around the flower stand. He provided some fun for the little boys in the group by letting them sit upon the huge black leather seat without the motor running, of course. The dream of owning a motorcycle was for sale that day, right along with the flowers. Every young boy who saw that man and his machine went home to dream of one day having such a toy for himself.

After wrapping the flowers and securing them with cellophane and ribbon, I handed them over to the young man, who seemed extremely pleased with his selection. His satisfaction was reflected in his eyes as they focused on the bright red glads nestled down in the wrapping paper. He again said, "This was my dad's favorite flower." He was holding the flowers in his arms as if the package were a small baby wrapped in a flannel blanket. I looked around to see that the crowd had left the bike, and everyone was now looking at the man holding the flowers because the look on his face was so compelling that it was difficult to turn away from him. It was if everyone were waiting to hear an explanation from this gentleman about his father and the flowers. He glanced up to find all of us staring at him, and that was when he said, "My father died many years ago, and he is buried in a local cemetery in this town. I drove here today to visit his gravesite because this is the anniversary of his death, and it was by accident that I came by the square on my way there. You will never know how happy I am to find his favorite flower here for me to take to his grave. When I was a child growing up in my father's house, he always grew gladiolus, and I have special memories of him out among his flowers. And today was like a trip back to my childhood. I realize that by the time I take these to his grave, they might not be in the best of shape, but I know my dad won't mind because he will be happy to have them resting on his marker."

He slowly moved to the motorcycle, sat upon the large seat and carefully positioned the wrapped bouquet below the clear windshield, hoping to offer as much protection as possible. He cranked the big motor and took off around the courthouse, leaving all of us standing there with warm feelings in our hearts, hoping that when we are no longer around, someone will bring our favorite flowers to rest on our grave markers. In our minds, we could imagine the scene at the cemetery with the motorcycle reverently cruising through the paths, coming to a stop at the dad's grave, and the man placing the flowers on top of the marble marker. We could see him in a few moments of reflection and maybe a little silent conversation about how he remembered his dad working in the gladiolus, and then maybe he would say a short, silent prayer before he left the place where his dad now rested. He would step away and back slowly to the Harley-Davidson, leaving the brilliant glads shining in the bright sun on the grave. Then we could imagine him steering the big machine back to the open road and taking off fast, accompanied by feelings of satisfaction and sadness.

A Few Facts About Gladiola

Common name: gladiola
Botanical name: *Gladiolus spp.*
Type: corm
Size: 2.5-3 feet tall
Origin: Southern Europe and South Africa
Soil: almost any kind
Light: sun or part shade
Description: The blooms are produced on long stalks

with many stacked flowers, which open sequentially from the bottom to the top of the plant. Sword-like foliage, which shoots up from the underground corm, grows rather profusely before the plant forms a blossom stalk. Because of the hybridization process, the blooms can be almost any color, and some are variegated.

Gladiola growing in the garden stand out and are very upright, just like the man on the Harley-Davidson. These flowers seem to know exactly what they want, and they make a clear-cut statement in the garden, as well as in the vase. The way the plants grow and the very vivid colors of the plants make every visitor to a garden stop and look at them, just the way people are compelled to stop and look at a sleek motorcycle when it comes by. Now when I see a motorcycle or a gladiola, I always think of the man who came to the square to buy his deceased father some flowers for his grave. There is something so heart-warming about this scenario that I find it hard to forget, and I always hope that when I am gone, someone will bring a few brilliant glads and lay them on top of my grave, especially if they rode on a motorcycle to get there.

The "Sister" Customer:
The Three Roses Lady

S he drove her large family sedan right up to the flower tables, so close that I thought she must be handicapped in some way and could not walk very far. She opened the car door, but she left the engine running. When she stepped from the car, I knew I was mistaken about her possible infirmity because she walked very briskly, right up to me, and spoke rather hurriedly. "I need three roses for my sister," she said. All the while she seemed very anxious and in a big rush. Almost before I could get the roses out of the bucket and get them wrapped, she was paying me for them and moving toward her car. Her manner and obvious anxiety were the reasons I took particular notice of her and would remember this first encounter for a long time. She was most polite and did not intrude in any way, but it was clear that she had a mission, as well as a problem with watching her time.

Maybe it wasn't the next Saturday morning, but some Saturday soon after our first meeting, she came again. She pulled the car up to the flower tables in the same fashion, left the motor running and bought the flowers with the same haste. It was about this time that I started to notice the routines of some of my regular customers and their attraction to certain flowers. Selling flowers directly to people, interacting across a card table at close range, gives the vendor a marvelous opportunity to know and observe personality traits, as well as the order of their priority lists. These personal characteristics would not be so easily spotted in another situation. There is something about a flower positioned between two people that brings out the need to share inner thoughts and personal agendas. Somewhere within this kind of communication I started to know that cut flowers did indeed have a sort of healing power. In my relationship with these Saturday morning customers, I came to know intuitively what a flower could do for them or for the person for whom they were buying the flower.

Certain Saturday mornings required more motivation than others for me to make it to the square: those mornings when the drizzle hid the sun, those mornings when the flower containers did not stand in place, and particularly those mornings when the whole endeavor was drawn into the shape of a question mark. A particular question—"Why are you doing this, going to all this trouble and effort?"—would rise at the same hour that I arose from my bed. The question always frightened me somewhat, but the answer was the scariest part of the interrogation. It certainly was not for the money because that was minimal compared to the work and trouble it took to pull off the Saturday morning endeavor. It was not that I needed to fill my time with some busywork because the farm provided enough of that for me and several other workers. The answer always came louder and clearer than I cared to acknowledge because of people like "The Sister Customer" and my need to have them know the joy of cut flowers. I knew my blooms were filling a need for them that ordinary florist flowers could not fill. These farm-fresh cut flowers had a message they liked, a message for someone special in their lives or a message to a deceased loved one. The appreciation I felt from these customers was never a vague or inadequate thing, but rather a profound and emphatic response. Maybe it wasn't even like a voice, but more like a wavelength the customer and I shared, knowing their gift of my flowers would express their innermost caring to their loved ones or friends. And so it was that almost every Saturday morning began with "why" and always ended with "thank goodness I was there."

The "Sister Customer" started to come to the square on a regular basis, but she always acted the same way and bought the same three roses. Finally we became such familiar associates that she felt comfortable carrying on a little small talk, not that she took any large amount of her time to do this, but she at least had a few words to say about ordinary things like the weather or such to me. Probably the strangest thing about her was how she zeroed in on those roses for her sister, ignoring huge displays of other flowers like bright sunflowers or zinnias. She had those roses in her line of focus almost before she stepped from her car.

Finally one day the worst happened. She came to make her purchase, and I had no roses. This happens sometimes when flowers are grown in the open fields, given the way nature operates with insects and bad weather. The disappointment that registered on her face broke my heart. It was at that moment that she told me her story. She explained that she came every Saturday to buy the three roses for her older sister who was dying with cancer. She went on to say that when the older sister became seriously ill, she had given up her own house in another town and moved in with the older sister to care for her. This day she took the time to tell me about how, quite by accident, she had stopped by the square the first time and bought the three roses from me to take home to her sister. Her sister had been so pleased that the Saturday routine became just that—a routine for her to stop by the square and buy the roses. And then she told me something I have never forgotten. She said she came to this strange town, having given up her other life, to look after her sick sister and to take over all the duties of the house and the regimen of caring for a seriously sick family member. Not a young woman herself, this younger sister told of looking after the grocery shopping, the bill paying, the maintenance of the house, and other daily chores, as well as taking full responsibility for her older sister's health needs. She spoke of numerous hospital and doctor visits, drugstore visits and all of the other full-time efforts that went along with caring for her ill sister. Her most poignant remark came when she told me about the roses—"It is the most amazing thing. I bathe my sister, take her to the doctor, give her medicine daily, clean her room and do everything I can to make her comfortable. The only thing that makes her smile is when I come in the door with the three roses and place them in a vase near her bed. You have no idea how much that one weak little smile means to me after trying everything I can to make her respond." She then went away empty-handed because no other flowers would do for her sister.

I decided that I would never be without roses again, even if I had to buy some from a wholesaler in a nearby large city. I did run out a few times, but I felt no regret in buying the imported kind of roses to take to the square for her because I could not handle her look of despair on hearing that I had no roses that Saturday. We both understood, but never said, that there would be a time, not too far off, when the roses would no longer be needed for the older sister. The horrible disease would take her away and leave the younger sister with great pain and desolation. However, her loss would be somewhat lessened when she thought of the smiles she had been able to bring to her sister's face with the three roses.

Not ever having had a sister, I had not given much thought to it until this kind lady came into my life. In fact, most of my life, I had been perfectly satisfied with being basically an only child since my brother was eight years older than I. Then I began to earnestly regret the fact that I had been born into a family with only an older brother as my sibling and wanted desperately to know the love and caring this lady had given her dying older sister. Knowing this lady gave me the opportunity to tell my three daughters the following Christmas about the two sisters. I wrote them a special kind of Christmas message relating all about the three roses and how the two sisters came to the end of their days with this special blessing of devotion. My daughters were not ever surprised to get this type of thing from me at Christmas, and they rather expected something along these lines, but I think years from now, that Christmas message will take on a new meaning for them. Age gives us the opportunity to remember some of our mother's little lessons about life and death.

A Few Facts About Roses

Common name: rose
Botanical name: *Rosa*
Soil: fertile and well-drained
Light: full sun
Origin: Asia
Types: erect, climbing or trailing shrubs
Description: The rose flower has served as a symbol of love, romance, perfection and elegance in its long history, becoming closely associated with the culture of many civilizations. It figures prominently in religion, customs, literature and legends, being found throughout history in paintings, embroidery, music and architecture. The Greek poetess Sappho calls the rose "the queen of flowers" in her "Ode to the Rose" and expresses the sentiment of the world —that almost everyone's favorite flower is the rose. For many centuries the rose or parts of it have been used for everything from medicine to perfume-making.

The dying sister's devotion to roses is symbolic of how the history of the rose has evolved over the centuries, meaning all things to all people. There is something rather magical about this ancient flower existing well before the Roman Empire, the way it was taken from country to country, and the way it was the "favorite flower" and still is the "favorite flower" all over the world. Maybe this very sick lady felt a special kinship with the flower not only for its beauty, but also because the history of the flower proves that life goes on and on, even when individuals pass on to another world.

The end of summer came, followed by an early frost, and I did not go to sell flowers again until the following spring. Every Saturday I looked anxiously for the younger sister to come for the three roses, fearing that the news would not be good. Sure enough, she did not come for many Saturdays. Then one day she returned. She no longer was in a hurry, and I knew that her sister must have died during the winter months. After a few hugs, a few tears and a little conversation, we agreed that her sister was extremely lucky to have had her to take such good care of her at the end of her life. She did not buy any flowers for herself. That was a ritual reserved for a special sister who had gone away. However, as she was leaving, I gave her my biggest and most spectacular arrangement of roses, explaining to her that she deserved them for being the best of all sisters.

The Little Girl:
Any Flower Will Do

A twelve-year-old girl is the epitome of all the horrors of adolescence, all the pimples on the face, the awkward arrangement of the body parts, and the unsure feeling that nothing is certain. It is that time when the baby in you is fading away and the grown-up in you is trying to break loose from underneath all that uncertainty. Adolescence is extraordinarily uncomfortable for both sexes, but I think it is more of a problem for girls because they always seemed to me to be more aware of their ungraceful state. Maybe it is the natural way that boys always have that masculine residue from their childhood, like the fishing, hunting and ball playing that helps them slide from childhood to adolescence with less difficulty than girls. Maybe the girl who is approaching her teen years is more aware of the fact that she must be chosen by the male rather than the other way around. Armed with the undesirable appearance and the uncertainty of what is coming, the girl must find a way to get over the transition without too much baggage following her to maturity.

Some Saturdays at the square were constantly busy, some were spasmodically busy, and some were not too busy at all. The particular Saturday an adolescent girl appeared was one of those Saturdays when the crowds came and went in rapid succession, making me very busy at times and not busy at all at other moments. Somehow she wedged herself in between one of those crowds and waited until she could get my attention. Then she moved to the edge of the flower table and very shyly asked how much the flowers sold for. I explained rather brusquely, without thinking and without looking up, that all individual flowers were sold at a dollar a stem, regardless of the kind of flower. Therefore, I explained, a zinnia and a rose would sell for the same price.

She walked from one end of the table to the other, looking intently at all the flowers, almost as if they were some sort of precious jewels. Her eyes glowed and a smile broke from her small well-formed lips as she took all the beauty in, as if storing it for sometime later. She did not ask any more questions, but moved slowly, absorbing through her eyes as much loveliness as possible. If ever I saw someone who could talk with flowers, it was this young girl. The appreciation she expressed through just her movement and the look of her eyes told a tale of love, a love founded totally on appreciation of beauty. It was as if her preteen clumsiness and discomfort were washed away by seeing all the flowers on display.

She was in such a state of pleasure that I thought she

might just stay there for the rest of the morning, but in a little while, she looked up and said she would be back in just a few minutes. At that moment, I asked her which kind of flower she might like to have. I will never forget her answer: "I would like to have any one of these flowers. I probably would have a hard time choosing one because I love them all." Before I could do anything else, she had disappeared across the parking area to the sidewalk around the courthouse building, where two adults stood waiting for her. I watched her as she was obviously trying to explain to them about the flowers, pointing to my flower tables, pleading her case with every gesture possible. Then the worst of all things happened. After a little while, the two adults turned in the opposite direction and started to walk away, shaking their heads. The young girl followed behind them, head bowed, walking very slowly and dejectedly. It was like one of those times in a bad dream when you can't scream; you open your mouth, and nothing comes out. I wanted to yell after her to come back, but I was too far away, and then they were gone. An opportunity had come my way, and I had let it slip away. It was not an intentional action on my part; it was more like something that happened so fast that it did not register in my mind what was really happening. But when she and her family turned the corner, I knew just what she was feeling.

I had been in her shoes, and even though it had been about fifty years before, those shoes still hurt. Not the shoes worn on feet, but the shoes of hard times, when flowers and such are a luxury item, not something that hard earned money can be wasted on.

Every Saturday after the young girl went away disappointed, I looked expectantly for her, hoping against hope she would come back to look at the flowers so I could give her any blooms she wanted. She never came again. I reasoned that maybe her family did not live near there, or maybe they were just passing through on a road trip, or maybe, worst of all, she knew she would not be able to buy flowers and was too embarrassed to come again. I prayed that that was not the case, and for the rest of the flower season, I looked for her at the square. Sometimes I would see an adolescent girl in a crowd some distance away and almost call out to her, shortly before realizing that it was not the same girl.

There was one good thing that came out of that experience. From that time forward, there was never a child of any age who came to look at flowers who went away empty-handed. I made sure that I never made that mistake again, that horrible mistake of having a child want a flower so very much and not be able to afford it. On certain days when I am haunted by the memory of the girl and her parents walking away from the square that Saturday, I satisfy myself with the thought that one day the little girl will grow up to have a garden filled with every kind of flower, and all she will have to do is walk out her door and pick whatever she wants. I am sure her hunger for the beauty that flowers express will serve her well, and she will grow to understand their healing power.

Barbara:
The Zinnia Lady

On an eastern corner directly across from the courthouse square sits a well-kept building that houses a drugstore. Barbara's husband's family has owned the corner drugstore for many years, so far back that the store still has a certain resemblance to an old-fashioned pharmacy, the kind that every town had before the superstore phenomenon took over the market. Years ago the neighborhood drugstore was an enchanted place to visit. In the era when the rest of the world of retail was not too concerned with glitz and glamour, the drugstore was where one could spend hours looking in the shiny glass counters, which housed everything from jewelry to clocks, or browse the special gift area filled with teddy bears and toys, and, of course, the perfume counter with its famous bath powders and colognes. All of this was in addition to the pharmacy in the back where the "druggist" practiced his own form of medicine and filled the prescriptions given by the real doctors. It was a time when most people relied on the drugstore remedy as much as they put faith in the physician's advice. Sometimes the pharmacist's remedy was used rather than the physician's advice, or certainly in some cases, both forms of advice were used together, with the sick person never considering one opinion better than the other. But the best part of the old-fashioned drugstore was the soda fountain, an area with bar stools and a high counter surrounding a space where a soda jerk made the most delicious milk shakes, banana splits, grilled cheese sandwiches, and other snacks. It was a real treat to get just a plain Coca-Cola in one of those special fountain glasses with Coca-Cola written on the side. But if you added a scoop of vanilla ice cream to this glass, it was truly a little taste of heaven. Sometimes you used a spoon, and sometimes a straw would do just fine, but either way, once that magic liquid got to your mouth, it was the best. It might be because these types of drinks had a "soda pop" base that the name of the area became known as the "soda fountain."

Modernity replaced these wonderful soda fountains with dull drink machines, and many of the other items in the old drugstores are no longer in inventory. However, what remained unchanged in Barbara's husband's pharmacy was advice, that much-valued opinion which could not be replaced by a superstore with no ties to the past and no small town manners. Because the local people in this small-town had trusted this medical advice for more than a generation, the more modern, large drugstores could never quite dislodge some of these loyal customers, even though their prices were somewhat lower and their inventory larger. Being greeted on a first-name basis and having a personal relationship with the clerks and the pharmacist gave customers a reason to stay with the old-time drugstore instead of going to the new stores.

On Saturday mornings the drugstore generally opened about the same time we got to the square, and since the people who worked there parked in the square area, we usually exchanged morning greetings and small talk about the flowers. Barbara's husband, coffee cup in hand, would often come by the flower table. He had been raised in a family with a great appreciation for flowers of all kinds, so it was no surprise that he, too, had this same love of beautiful blossoms. This man was quite possibly the neatest and most clean-cut individual I had ever met, possessing a manner and personality that complemented his physical appearance. As he made his way through the parking lot to the store across the street, he usually stopped by to check out the inventory of fresh flowers for the day. He would not buy at that time, but he would either come back later or call someone when he got to the store and tell that person to come see me.

This man seemed to have a real passion for zinnias, and I soon learned why this was true. His wife, Barbara, was the reason. She was just as neat and clean-cut looking as he, and together they could be the poster children for the "Neat Society," if there were such an organization. But the most amazing thing about her was her sunny personality, which never varied, no matter the time of day, or the week, or the year. The speed with which she moved, the bright smile and the staccato manner of speaking all came together in this pleasant and neat person to form what might be called "sunshine" walking around in the body of a human. Although she exuded the "so much to do and so little time to do it" persona, her real sense of caring and concern always overshadowed that hurried appearance. Most of the time when she came to the square, she would leave her car running, jump out, run around to the zinnias, make her selection and be on her way in a matter of minutes, never wasting time standing around talking with other customers or with me. But amazingly, after she was gone, no one had the sense that she had not given anyone the proper greeting or the correct amount of attention. It was just the opposite. Most people commented about how nice she was, or made some other complimentary remark; no one offered any form of criticism about the way she busily went about her day.

This lady truly loved zinnias and bought them for others and for herself, giving them to someone who was ill or just taking them to someone who was having a difficult day.

Sometimes her husband would buy roses for his mother, but he always checked on the zinnia inventory early in the day so that he could get a few for his wife. On the Saturday before Mother's Day, he came by to purchase some flowers for his mother and for his wife, but, in addition, he noticed that I had made some very small arrangements in seashells. My youngest daughter had made an early spring visit to a secluded beach and picked up lots of shells, which she shared with me, realizing that I would probably make flower arrangements in them. My children had grown up in my house knowing that I would put flowers in almost any kind of object that had an opening for them. During the summer when squash were in season, I took advantage of those large vegetables, the ones that got left on the vine too long, scooped out the centers, and stuck a few flowers in them. A bright yellow squash filled with a tiny bit of greenery, like rosemary, and two or three small zinnias made an irresistible arrangement for the nursing home resident or a token gift for anyone. So graduating from the squash to the large conch shell was no stretch for my drunken creative mind. I had the idea of using some of these shells for very small arrangements on Mother's Day because sometimes children need a present that isn't too large in price or size. So when I was making the arrangements the Friday before Mother's Day, I included a few large conch shells with small flowers and greenery filling the openings. They were a big hit.

When Barbara's husband came by the square that Mother's Day weekend, he asked me to save one of these shell arrangements for him along with his other flowers. This couple had two children, a boy and a girl. The parents certainly seemed to put a lot of effort into the child-rearing process along with a huge amount of parental interest in every activity in which these children were engaged. The daughter was away at college, and the boy was still at home going to high school around this time. In most families, mothers share a special bond with their sons. The following story substantiates that belief and shows how gratitude within the family is a shared thing as well as a pretty good adhesive.

Barbara came by the square one Saturday shortly after Mother's Day and in a rather unusual fashion for her asked me to sit down to talk because she had something special to tell me. The fact that she would take the time to sit caused me to think that what she was going to tell me was out-of-the-ordinary. She said, "On Saturday night before Mother's Day Sunday, my son was out with some friends until rather late, but when he returned, he came into my room and asked me to come into the kitchen for a minute. When I went there, he brought out a seashell filled with tiny flowers and said that he could not wait until the next day to tell me what a special mother I am, and that he wanted me to have the shell that night, rather than waiting until the next day." She went on to tell me how impressed she was that he had come by and selected something so special for her, and that she was going to keep the seashell forever.

I did not tell Barbara that her husband was responsible for getting the gift for her son to give to her. Probably the two of them had discussed it previously, and a decision had been made for the dad to get the flowers from me because he was going to be at the drugstore anyway. It really doesn't matter about the logistics. The most important thing about it was that her husband and her son had a common message to convey, and their working together to have this happen made the gift even more special, especially in my eyes.

A Few Facts About Zinnias

Common name: zinnia, old maid
Botanical name: *Zinnia sp.*
Type: annual
Size: 6 inches to 3 feet tall
Origin: Mexico
Light: full sun

Soil: well-drained

Growth rate: moderate

Description: These flowers were introduced into Europe from Mexico in the eighteenth century, having been grown by Montezuma's gardeners and their Aztec ancestors for many years before. The name "zinnia" comes from the German botanist Joann Gottfried Zinn. Even though some people called them "old maids" years ago in this country, these flowers are enjoyed by the young and old alike today. In its original form, the zinnia was a dull lavender, but within the last one hundred and fifty years, zinnias have been bred to form many colors and sizes. Zinnias are among the best flowers for cutting purposes, having a long vase life and requiring little maintenance in the garden.

There was something about Barbara that made me think of a zinnia rather than merely the fact that she was in love with the flower. The way she looked and moved, that "sunshine" personality, her bright and bubbly style—all these qualities reminded me of a long row of multicolored zinnias. She knew, without a doubt, that a large bouquet of these brightly colored flowers could solve all the problems of the depressed, the sick and the grief-stricken, and if there were a celebration, the flowers could only enhance the spirit of the occasion. Zinnias are unmistakably the universal cure, at least in Barbara's eyes.

The Other Zinnia Lady:
The Edible Zinnias

The slightly gray-haired man and the middle-aged woman strolled very slowly around the square, looking at each vendor's goods, making light conversation with other customers and with the vendors themselves. Their faces seemed to be kind but showed a certain sadness and look of concern, as if they had endured pain of a special nature, making the idea of walking around with smiles on their lips fairly difficult. Most of the time they had with them a young girl who appeared to be about nine or ten years old, not the proper age to be their child, but most probably a grandchild. Unlike the couple with whom she walked, the girl seemed happy and full of energy—a total misfit with the two adults. She bounced from one vendor's stall to the next, asking questions, making conversation and generally having a great time.

My first experience with the three of them set the stage for all of their future visits. As the older lady approached the table, her sad eyes became transfixed on the large bucket of zinnias, and her gaze never left them to go to any other flowers. I noticed the change in her eyes as she looked at the mass of vivid colors in the zinnia bucket, and almost instantaneously, the sad look was replaced by a soft, glad stare. Her husband was standing off to the side as if thinking that should he come too close, he might somehow be entangled in the flowers. As she fingered the blossoms, he made a slightly demanding comment: "Don't buy anything you can't eat!" He was standing so far away that at first, I did not realize the two of them were together. The young child quickly moved to the lady's side, and the two of them began picking their favorite color zinnias from the bucket. It was as if they did not even hear the admonishment from the man standing off in the distance. It took the two of them quite a while to carefully select their favorite colors because they disagreed on some of their individual favorites. However, after two or three flowers were selected, the woman handed them to me to wrap and said, "I need just a few flowers for my kitchen table because I want to just sit and look at them when I can." Her husband moved from the sidelines and produced the right amount of money to pay for the flowers. He did not remind her of his demand not to buy them, nor did he seem to mind the fact that she had spent money. He simply stepped up to the situation and seemed okay with it.

The next Saturday they were back, and this time Glenn was ready for him. Before the older man could reach our flower tables, Glenn shouted out to him, "We have some zinnias that taste just like steak today, and our roses taste just like ham!" The man knew exactly what we were referring to, and a broad smile broke across his face. It was then that we both knew we had misjudged his personality the Saturday before when he had told his wife not to buy anything she could not eat. He was one of those men who wanted everyone to think he was a big, hostile, gruff person with no heart, when in actuality, he had teddy bear insides. Our claim that the flowers were edible broke the ice and led to a ritual of sorts every Saturday. It was as if the man looked forward to hearing our proclamation about edible flowers and approached the area with an expectant look on his face every time he came to the square.

Sometimes the lady was not with him. When we asked him about her, he said she wasn't feeling well or was a bit under the weather. He further explained about her back pain or leg pain, and then I just knew there was something bothering him that was painful to discuss. On these occasions, he would hang around, talk with us and not buy any flowers. At other times, the young girl came with him, and she would buy a few flowers for her grandmother who wasn't feeling well. Somehow I knew the lady must have other problems that were not just physical, but maybe that kind of problem that worries the mind and makes the body wish it could live somewhere else with different circumstances.

Then one day a car driven by a woman I had never seen before came up to the flower tables. I did recognize the person in the passenger seat. It was the little girl who had come with her grandparents many times before. The woman and the little girl got out of the car and bought several zinnias for the ailing lady who was unable to come to the square. After they had completed their shopping, one of the regular vendors at the square told me that the unknown lady driving the car was the mother of the young girl who was always with her grandparents. This regular vendor explained the family dynamics that had to do with a court case involving custody of the young girl, who was always with her grandparents except for today, when she had come with her mother. It seemed that years before, the couple's daughter was part of several bad situations and had lived a life that was unacceptable for child-rearing in the eyes of the court. Therefore, the grandparents were awarded permanent custody of the child. I suddenly understood all the pain in the faces of the couple and the reason the lady needed to have a few brightly colored zinnias on her kitchen table. As much pain as she had endured, she knew exactly how to heal some of her hurt by just having two or three flowers to look at. It occurred to me that even with her worrisome circumstances she was better off than some because her coping mechanisms were better than most.

Some days when the temperature stayed around one hundred degrees, the insects biting every exposed area of my body and a back aching from hours of cutting flowers, I thought of the lady who needed the "edible zinnias," and it all seemed worthwhile.

Closing The Garden Gate
At Chinaberry Ranch

Of all the products one might sell, flowers are the best. There is no downside to selling flowers because everyone loves them, with the exception of a few weird folks and some people with allergies. Even these exceptions can be caught looking longingly at beautiful flowers on occasion. The field-grown flowers like the ones we raise at Chinaberry Ranch are the best because they have that just-picked look that most everyone loves. In fact, I suspect some people might just claim that they did grow them once they have them in their possession, which is fine with me. I care only that someone wants and appreciates them. I probably learned more about human nature while selling flowers directly to the customers here at the farm and at the square than in any other situation I have been exposed to in my life.

I became aware of the magic of a large display of fresh flowers when people passing by stopped to chat and lingered longer than they needed to. It was as if they hated to leave the beauty, fragrance and joy that the flowers radiated. Once a nice lady came just to chat and stayed a long time simply talking about planting certain seeds and how she had little luck with her zinnias. I went into great detail about the planting, spraying, fertilizing and other aspects of how to grow zinnias. She listened intently, and when I had finished my tutorial, she smiled wryly and said, "Actually the worst problem I have is getting around to taking the seeds out of paper envelope on the table. They will not grow sitting in the paper wrap." After a while I thought she must be joking with me. I, who thought nothing of planting hundreds of seeds on a daily basis, realized the problem was one that many people have—that problem of just starting a project like a garden. The love of fresh flowers, I have found, in most cases is not limited to those of us who plant and raise them. Some of my most eager customers were those who could not begin to grow anything and, as a result, seemed to have a greater appreciation of fresh flowers. There was the ever-present conversation about the "Green Thumb" and whether one had one or not. It was interesting to me that there were usually two categories of customers: those who swore that they did not have a green thumb and those who said they had flowers just like mine in their gardens. This latter group never mentioned anything about the green thumb, but the ones who could not grow flowers always seemed to blame their problem on not possessing that colorful digit. I always assured them that any person who is in the business of growing things would certainly have at least a small amount of brown dirt under that thumb. Brown, not green, was the color to look for in the growers group.

An individual's uniqueness is somehow made more obvious in the presence of flowers. An emotional bridge can be built between people with all kinds of differences when flowers are added to the mix. Flowers can be used to express sorrow and sympathy at funerals, as well as joy and exuberance at celebrations. They help us tell our family and friends how much we appreciate them and their endeavors, in addition to helping us make up for our mistakes. If I had not sold flowers, I would have never known that men love flowers just as much as women, if not more than women do. I would have never experienced the true value of the healing powers of cut flowers if I had not seen the look on those faces of old ladies and very young children when they held just a few flowers in their hands.

Sunsets are very special here at Chinaberry Ranch with the open sky affording a clear view of the setting sun sinking into the multicolored clouds surrounding it. As I sit, my rocking chair barely moving on the front porch at the end of the day, I often think of all those faces I have seen across the tables filled with different kinds and different colors of flowers, and I thank life for providing me the opportunity to experience those wonderful moments when I gave these people something that healed their hurt or lessened their pain. If I had another chance to live my life over again, I would not want to leave out this chapter, the chapter about growing, picking and selling fresh cut flowers to other people because the joy I received from this experience made my days seem worthwhile, even if little else seemed to make much difference.

As a result of my cut flower business, I became known as "The Flower Lady," and my real name faded into the unknown in the minds of many people in Sandersville and Dublin. Even a few years later, now that I have quit doing the flowers, some people still call me by that name, which always brings a smile to my face. It is a legacy I would not want to change.

Chinaberry Ranch
(Eleven Years Later)

If you drove up the driveway of Chinaberry Ranch today, it would be a very different experience from the drive eleven years ago. The driveway itself has been graded and covered with gravel. All the memories of the slick mud, deep ruts, unsightly ground and fear of sliding off the road are a thing of the past, and we rarely remember the pain and suffering of leaving a car at the bottom of the hill and proceeding to carry groceries and packages up the steep slope to the house. Whereas in the beginning of the ranch, the view was limited by overgrown brush, vines and debris of all kinds, the view today is best described as "you can see for a mile."

After you have driven to the top of the hill, gotten out of the car and looked around at the great view, you would see an airstrip and airplane hangar, an array of flower gardens in every size and shape, small vegetable gardens everywhere, a regulation two-hole golf course with sand bunkers, seven acres of pearl millet, a beautiful hardwood forest surrounding the property, and a bright yellow house reining over all this from eight feet above the ground. I have laughingly said that we have everything here with the exception of a Ferris wheel.

This place is an accumulation of dreams rather than a well-planned blueprint for the proper way to do things. It is more about taking something of little value and making it into something you love and being able to appreciate the process that got you here even more than the results. The most interesting part of the place is that it is forever changing because of the constant dreaming of the owners. For instance, our latest project is the making of ethanol as an alternative fuel for our cars. It did not occur to us that this process would be impossible or even difficult, and so we jumped in with both feet and have been busy doing that "research and development" thing that Glenn just loves. This is why we have seven acres of pearl millet planted alongside the airstrip and behind the house. We plan to grind, ferment and distill the product to make ethanol.

What's next? Who knows? Maybe we will dig a small pond at the bottom of the airstrip. One thing is for sure— the dreams never stop, and therefore Chinaberry Ranch is forever undergoing change.

At the end of a busy day, the rockers on the front porch are where we find our weary bodies resting, while the western sky provides us with a panoramic view of the setting sun. Sometimes we talk about our projects and the successes, and sometimes we discuss some of the mistakes we have made, but most of the time, we laugh. A life filled with dreams and laughter is a life worth living and living and living....